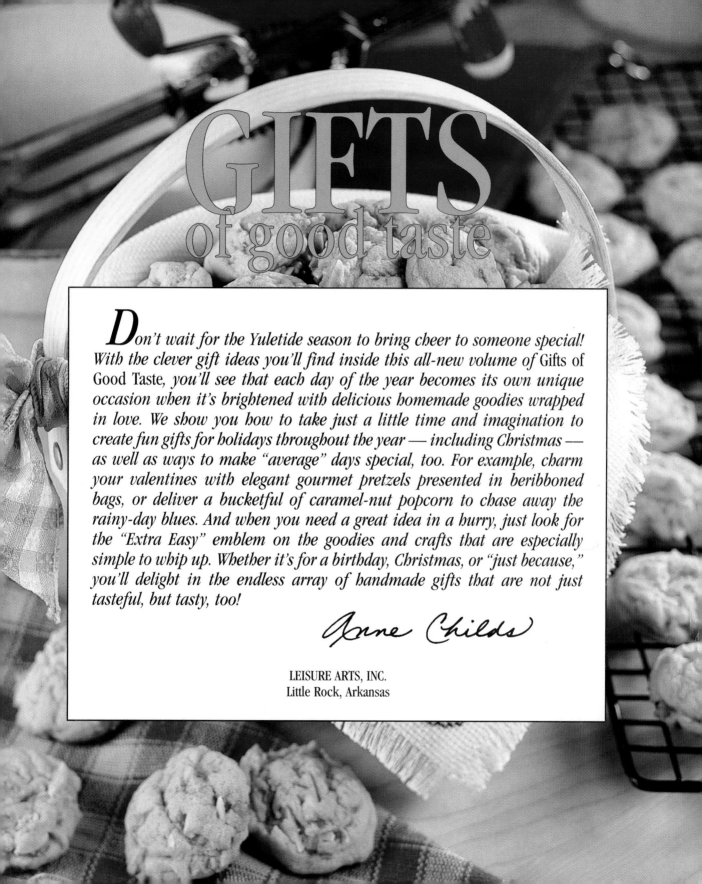

GIFTS
of good taste

*D*on't wait for the Yuletide season to bring cheer to someone special! With the clever gift ideas you'll find inside this all-new volume of Gifts of Good Taste, *you'll see that each day of the year becomes its own unique occasion when it's brightened with delicious homemade goodies wrapped in love. We show you how to take just a little time and imagination to create fun gifts for holidays throughout the year — including Christmas — as well as ways to make "average" days special, too. For example, charm your valentines with elegant gourmet pretzels presented in beribboned bags, or deliver a bucketful of caramel-nut popcorn to chase away the rainy-day blues. And when you need a great idea in a hurry, just look for the "Extra Easy" emblem on the goodies and crafts that are especially simple to whip up. Whether it's for a birthday, Christmas, or "just because," you'll delight in the endless array of handmade gifts that are not just tasteful, but tasty, too!*

Anne Childs

LEISURE ARTS, INC.
Little Rock, Arkansas

GIFTS
of good taste

EDITORIAL STAFF

Vice President and Editor-in-Chief: Anne Van Wagner Childs
Executive Director: Sandra Graham Case
Design Director: Patricia Wallenfang Sowers
Test Kitchen Director/Foods Editor: Celia Fahr Harkey, R.D.
Editorial Director: Susan Frantz Wiles
Publications Director: Kristine Anderson Mertes
Creative Art Director: Gloria Bearden
Senior Graphics Art Director: Melinda Stout

DESIGN
Designers: Sandra Spotts Ritchie, Anne Pulliam Stocks, Linda Diehl Tiano, and Cherece Athy Watson
Executive Assistants: Debra Smith and Billie Steward
Design Assistant: Melanie Vaughan

FOODS
Assistant Foods Editor: Jane Kenner Prather
Test Kitchen Home Economist: Rose Glass Klein
Test Kitchen Coordinator: Nora Faye Taylor
Test Kitchen Assistants: Camille T. Alstadt and Melissa Adams

TECHNICAL
Managing Editor: Barbara McClintock Vechik
Senior Technical Writer: Jennifer L. Hobbs

Technical Writers: Susan McManus Johnson and Theresa Hicks Young
Technical Associates: Laura Lee Powell, Marley N. Washum, and Susan Frazier

EDITORIAL
Managing Editor: Linda L. Trimble
Senior Associate Editor: Terri Leming Davidson
Associate Editor: Stacey Robertson Marshall
Assistant Editor: Janice Teipen Wojcik

ART
Book/Magazine Graphics Art Director: Diane Thomas
Senior Production Graphics Artist: Michael A. Spigner
Color Technician: Mark A. Hawkins
Photography Stylist: Karen Smart Hall
Publishing Systems Administrator: Cynthia M. Lumpkin
Publishing Systems Assistants: Susan Mary Gray and Myra S. Means

PROMOTIONS
Managing Editor: Alan Caudle
Associate Editor: Steven M. Cooper
Designer: Dale Rowett
Art Director: Linda Lovette Smart

BUSINESS STAFF

Publisher: Rick Barton
Vice President and General Manager: Thomas L. Carlisle
Vice President, Finance: Tom Siebenmorgen
Vice President, Retail Marketing: Bob Humphrey
Vice President, National Accounts: Pam Stebbins
Retail Marketing Director: Margaret Sweetin
General Merchandise Manager: Cathy Laird

Vice President, Operations: Brian U. Davis
Distribution Director: Rob Thieme
Retail Customer Service Director: Tonie B. Maulding
Retail Customer Service Managers: Carolyn Pruss and Wanda Price
Print Production Manager: Fred F. Pruss

Library of Congress Catalog Number 98-67372
International Standard Book Number 1-57486-133-6

10 9 8 7 6 5 4 3 2

Table of Contents

PEANUT BUTTER PARTY PACKS

Whether it's a birthday party or New Year's revelry, these fun favors will have guests tooting their own horns! Fill easy-to-make party cones with our rich, chocolaty Peanut Butter-Fruit Balls and party horns, then let the merriment begin.

PEANUT BUTTER-FRUIT BALLS

  1 cup smooth peanut butter
 1/2 cup honey
  1 cup quick-cooking oats
  1 cup confectioners sugar
  1 package (6 ounces) dried fruit bits
 1/2 cup frozen sweetened grated
       coconut
 12 ounces chocolate candy coating,
       chopped
  6 ounces semisweet baking
       chocolate, chopped

In a large bowl, beat peanut butter and honey until smooth. Add oats, confectioners sugar, dried fruit, and coconut; stir until well blended. Shape teaspoonfuls of candy into balls. Transfer to a baking sheet lined with waxed paper. Chill 2 hours.

In a heavy medium saucepan, melt candy coating and baking chocolate over low heat. Remove from heat (if chocolate begins to harden, return to heat). Removing about 12 candies at a time from refrigerator, dip candies into chocolate. Transfer candies to a baking sheet lined with waxed paper. Drizzle remaining chocolate over candies. Chill 30 minutes or until chocolate hardens. Store in an airtight container in refrigerator.

Yield: about 5½ dozen candies

PARTY PACKS

For each pack, you will need string, pencil, thumbtack, 8½" x 11" sheet of colored card stock, spray adhesive, wrapping paper, hot glue gun, decorative cellophane bag, curling ribbon, and a party horn.

1. For cone, tie one end of string around pencil. Insert thumbtack through string 7" from pencil. Insert tack into one corner of card stock. Holding tack in place and keeping string taut, mark curved line; cut out along drawn line.
2. Apply spray adhesive to wrong side of wrapping paper; glue to card stock shape. Cut paper even with edges of cut shape. Overlapping edges 1¼", glue straight edges together to form cone.
3. Place bag in cone and candy in bag. Tie several lengths of curling ribbon around top of bag; curl ends.
4. Place horn in cone.

NEIGHBORLY WELCOME

*H*elp a family settle into the neighborhood with this doubly delightful offering. A hearty entree, Easy Tamale Pie will provide a welcome break from all that unpacking. Top the pan with a cute collage of helpful hints — such as who's got the best take-out food and where to go for a good haircut!

EASY TAMALE PIE

1¹/₄ pounds ground beef
¹/₂ cup chopped onion
 1 clove garlic, minced
 1 can (11 ounces) Mexican-style whole kernel corn, drained
 1 can (8 ounces) tomato sauce
 1 can (4 ounces) chopped green chiles
 1 teaspoon chili powder
¹/₂ teaspoon salt
¹/₂ cup sour cream
 1 egg
 2 cups (8 ounces) shredded Cheddar cheese, divided
 1 package (6 ounces) Mexican-style corn bread mix and ingredients to prepare corn bread

Preheat oven to 375 degrees. In a large skillet, cook ground beef, onion, and garlic over medium-high heat until meat is brown and onion is tender; drain. Reduce heat to medium-low. Stir in corn, tomato sauce, green chiles, chili powder, and salt. Remove from heat.

In a small bowl, beat sour cream and egg until well blended. Stir in 1 cup cheese. Combine sour cream mixture with ground beef mixture. Spoon into a lightly greased 8³/₈ x 12³/₈ x 1¹/₈-inch aluminum foil baking pan with plastic lid. In a medium bowl, prepare corn bread mix according to package directions. Spread corn bread batter over casserole. Sprinkle with remaining 1 cup cheese. Bake uncovered 25 to 30 minutes or until mixture is heated through and corn bread topping is golden brown. Serve warm.

Yield: 6 to 8 servings

CASSEROLE PAN TOPPER

You will need a covered pan (from recipe, this page), assorted colors of construction paper, craft glue, tracing paper, and a black permanent fine-point marker.

1. For background, cut a 7¹/₂" x 11" piece from blue paper; cut across each corner ³/₄" from edge.

2. For grass, cut a strip of green paper 1¹/₂" x 11"; fold one long edge over ¹/₂". Make ¹/₂" cuts ¹/₈" apart along opposite edge of strip. Glue folded edge of strip along one long edge of background. Trim ends of grass even with background.

3. For buildings, cut four 2" x 2¹/₄" pieces from paper; glue to background.

4. Trace patterns, page 104, onto tracing paper; cut out. Use patterns to cut four roofs, one sun, one tree, and four clouds from construction paper; glue to background.

5. Use marker to write message on sun and on each building and to draw "stitches" along edges of tree and around message on sun. Glue background to top of lid.

HEAVENLY CHERRY CAKE

CHERRY VALENTINE CAKE

CAKE
- 3/4 cup butter or margarine, softened
- 1 1/2 cups sugar
- 2 cups all-purpose flour
- 2 teaspoons baking powder
- 1/8 teaspoon salt
- 3/4 cup milk
- 2 teaspoons clear vanilla extract
- 5 large egg whites
- 1/2 teaspoon cream of tartar

FILLING
- 1 jar (10 ounces) red maraschino cherries
- 2 cups confectioners sugar
- 1 package (3 ounces) cream cheese, softened
- 2 tablespoons butter or margarine, softened

ICING
- 1 1/2 cups sugar
- 3 tablespoons reserved cherry syrup
- 2 tablespoons water
- 2 egg whites
- 1 tablespoon light corn syrup
- 1/4 teaspoon cream of tartar
- 1 teaspoon clear vanilla extract

Preheat oven to 350 degrees. For cake, grease three 8-inch round cake pans and line bottoms with waxed paper; grease waxed paper. In a large bowl, cream butter and sugar until fluffy. In a small bowl, combine flour, baking powder, and salt. Alternately beat dry ingredients and milk into creamed mixture, beating until well blended. Stir in vanilla. In a large bowl, beat egg whites and cream of tartar until stiff peaks form; fold into batter. Pour batter into prepared pans. Bake 15 to 20 minutes or until a toothpick inserted in center of cake comes out clean. Cool in pans 10 minutes. Remove from pans and cool completely on a wire rack.

For filling, drain cherries, reserving 3 tablespoons syrup for icing. Chop cherries; place on paper towels and pat dry. Combine confectioners sugar, cream cheese, and butter in a medium bowl; beat until smooth. Stir in cherries. Spread filling between layers. (Filled layers can be stored in an airtight container in refrigerator until ready to ice.)

For icing, combine sugar, reserved cherry syrup, water, egg whites, corn syrup, and cream of tartar in top of a double boiler. Beat with an electric mixer until sugar is well blended. Place over boiling water; beat about 7 minutes or until soft peaks form. Remove from heat and add vanilla. Continue beating 2 minutes longer or until icing is desired consistency. Spread icing on top and sides of cake. Store in an airtight container in refrigerator.

Yield: 12 to 14 servings

PRETTY AND PINK CAKE TOPPER

You will need a white 4" heart-shaped doily, spray adhesive, pink card stock, gold fine-point paint pen, angel sticker, 1 yd. of 2"w sheer ribbon with gold edge, white craft wire, wire cutters, hot glue gun, 3/4" gold heart charm, and an 8" wooden skewer.

1. Cut heart from center of doily. Apply spray adhesive to wrong side of doily; glue to card stock. Cut out along outer edges of doily.
2. Use paint pen to highlight designs on doily; allow to dry. Apply sticker to doily.
3. Use ribbon and follow *Making a Bow,* page 121, to make a bow with four 4" loops and two 4 1/2" streamers; notch ends.
4. Hot glue charm to knot of bow, bow to top of skewer, and doily to skewer.

CUPID'S CANDY

Crunchy, creamy, and cool — these chocolate-mint squares are a luscious Valentine's treat! A beribboned spray adds a sweet touch to a jar of the candy.

DOUBLE CHOCOLATE PEPPERMINT CRUNCH

  1 package (6 ounces) white baking chocolate, chopped

  6 ounces vanilla candy coating, chopped

$1/2$ cup finely crushed peppermint candies

  4 ounces bittersweet baking chocolate, chopped

Line an 8-inch square baking pan with aluminum foil, extending foil over 2 sides of pan; grease foil. In top of a double boiler, combine white baking chocolate and candy coating over hot, not simmering, water; stir until mixture melts. Stir in crushed peppermint candies. Pour mixture into prepared pan. Chill about 20 minutes or until firm.

In a small saucepan, melt bittersweet chocolate over low heat. Spread evenly over candy. Chill about 30 minutes or until chocolate hardens. Use ends of foil to lift candy from pan. Cut into 1-inch squares. Store in an airtight container in refrigerator.

Yield: about 4 dozen pieces candy

CUPID JAR TOPPER

You will need 20" of 2"w sheer ribbon, 18" each of two coordinating colors of $1/8$"w satin ribbon and gold cord, glass container with knobbed lid (we used a 4" dia. x 7"h crystal biscuit jar), hot glue gun, cherub charm, two silk rosebuds, and artificial baby's breath.

For tag, you will *also* need tracing paper, decorative-edge craft scissors, card stock, black permanent fine-point marker, $1/8$" dia. hole punch, and 10" of $1/16$"w satin ribbon.

1. Tie ribbons and cord into bows around knob of lid; knot cord ends.

2. Glue cherub, rosebuds, and baby's breath to center of bows.

3. For tag, trace heart pattern, page 104, onto tracing paper. Use pattern and craft scissors to cut heart from card stock. Use marker to write message on tag. Punch hole in tag. Use ribbon to attach tag to knob of lid.

SWEETHEART PRETZEL STICKS

*S*ay "I love you" with
Gourmet Pretzels that you can
make at home! Our treats are
doubly delicious because they're
double-dipped — first in
caramel and nuts, then in
chocolate. Deliver them in
cellophane bags tied with ribbon
and chenille-stem hearts for a
sweetheart of a presentation.

GOURMET PRETZELS

  1 package (14 ounces) caramels
  3 tablespoons water
 18 large pretzel sticks (about
      6¹⁄₂ inches long)
  1 cup chopped pecans, toasted and
      coarsely ground
  1 package (6 ounces) semisweet
      chocolate chips
  6 ounces chocolate candy coating,
      chopped
  4 ounces white baking chips
  4 ounces vanilla candy coating,
      chopped

Line a baking sheet with waxed paper; grease waxed paper. Combine caramels and water in a heavy medium saucepan over low heat. Stirring frequently, cook about 15 minutes or until mixture is smooth. Holding each pretzel over saucepan, spoon caramel over two-thirds of pretzel. Roll in pecans and place on prepared baking sheet. Chill about 15 minutes or until caramel sets.

Melt chocolate chips and chocolate candy coating in a heavy medium saucepan over low heat. Remove from heat (if chocolate begins to harden, return to heat). Drizzle chocolate mixture over caramel-coated area of pretzels. Chill about 10 minutes or until chocolate hardens.

Melt baking chips and vanilla candy coating in a heavy small saucepan over low heat. Remove from heat (if mixture begins to harden, return to heat). Drizzle vanilla mixture over chocolate-coated area of pretzels. Chill about 10 minutes or until coating hardens. Store in an airtight container in a cool place.

Yield: 18 pretzels

SWEETHEART GIFT BAGS

For each gift bag, you will need a red chenille stem, white and silver curling ribbon, 16" of ⁵⁄₈"w white satin ribbon, and a cellophane bag (we used a 4" x 10¹⁄₂" bag).

1. Beginning 3" from one end, shape stem into a heart shape (Fig. 1); twist to secure.

Fig. 1

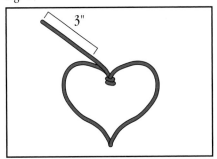

2. Knot three lengths of curling ribbon around stem at top of heart; curl ribbon ends. Tie satin ribbon into a bow around knot; notch ribbon ends.
3. Place gift in bag. Wrap end of stem around top of bag to secure.

COOKIE KEEPER

*D*oes everyone say you and your best friend are two of a kind? Celebrate your "cookie-cutter" friendship with this fun and practical gift! Filled with heart-shaped Cherry Bit Cookies for munching, the homey embellished container becomes a handy keeper for organizing cookie-making supplies once it's empty.

CHERRY BIT COOKIES

1¼ cups butter or margarine, softened
2¼ cups sugar
2 eggs
1½ teaspoons vanilla extract
1 teaspoon cherry flavoring
4½ cups all-purpose flour
1 teaspoon baking powder
¾ teaspoon salt
1 jar (10 ounces) maraschino cherries, finely chopped and well drained

In a large bowl, cream butter and sugar until fluffy. Add eggs, vanilla, and cherry flavoring; beat until smooth. In a medium bowl, combine flour, baking powder, and salt. Add dry ingredients to creamed mixture; stir until a soft dough forms. Stir in cherries. Divide dough into fourths and wrap in plastic wrap; chill 2 hours.

Preheat oven to 350 degrees. On a lightly floured surface, use a floured rolling pin to roll out one fourth of dough to ⅛-inch thickness. Use a 4-inch-wide heart-shaped cookie cutter to cut out cookies. Transfer to an ungreased baking sheet. Bake 8 to 10 minutes or until bottoms are lightly browned. Transfer cookies to a wire rack to cool. Repeat with remaining dough. Store in an airtight container.

Yield: about 3½ dozen cookies

"COOKIE CUTTERS" CONTAINER

You will need a container with lid (we used an 8" square by 8½"h plastic container), poster board, paper-backed fusible web, fabric to cover poster board, 4"w heart-shape cookie cutter, fabric for appliqués, black permanent fine-point marker, and a hot glue gun.

1. Measure around container; add ½". Cut a piece of poster board 5" by the determined measurement. Leaving 2" between shapes, draw around poster board two times each on fusible web and wrong side of fabric. Cut one web piece and one fabric piece 1" outside drawn lines. Cut remaining web piece and fabric piece ¼" inside drawn lines. Follow manufacturer's instructions to fuse each web piece to wrong side of same-size fabric piece. Do not remove paper backing from smaller fabric piece.
2. Place poster board at center of wrong side of larger fabric piece. Fold corners of fabric diagonally over corners of poster board; fuse in place. Fold long, then short edges of fabric over poster board; fuse in place. Remove paper backing from smaller fabric piece; fuse to wrong side of fabric-covered poster board.
3. Using cookie cutter as a pattern, follow *Making Appliqués*, page 122, to make two heart appliqués from appliqué fabric. Arrange appliqués on right side of fabric-covered poster board; fuse in place.
4. Use marker to write "COOKIE CUTTERS" on appliqués, outline edges, and to draw "stitches" across outer edges of appliqués.
5. Overlapping short ends in back, glue fabric-covered poster board around container.

ZESTY PRETZEL SNACKS

*F*riends and "leprechauns" alike will love these zesty Garlic-Parmesan Pretzels! They're a cinch to make, and it takes no time to decorate a plastic jar with a clever clover tag and ribbon. What a super way to ring in St. Paddy's Day!

GARLIC-PARMESAN PRETZELS

- 2 packages (10 ounces each) small pretzel twists
- 1/2 cup vegetable oil
- 2 packages (1.2 ounces each) Caesar salad dressing mix

Preheat oven to 250 degrees. Place pretzels in a large roasting pan. Use an electric mixer to combine oil and salad dressing mix in a small bowl. Pour oil mixture over pretzels; stir until well coated. Bake 30 minutes, stirring after 15 minutes. Spread on aluminum foil to cool. Store in an airtight container.

Yield: about 14 cups pretzels

ST. PADDY'S PRETZEL JAR

You will need tracing paper, white poster board, black permanent fine-point marker, three 12" green chenille stems, wire cutters, hot glue gun, 1"w ribbon, and a two-quart green plastic jar.

1. Trace pattern, page 104, onto tracing paper; cut out. Use pattern to cut shamrock from poster board. Use marker to draw "stitches" along edges of shamrock.
2. Cut three 9" lengths and one 3" length from chenille stems.
3. Leaving 1" at one end untwisted, twist ends of one 9" length together (Fig. 1). Fold twisted portion to front to form

pretzel. Wrap 1/4" of each end to back of pretzel to secure. Repeat using remaining 9" lengths. Glue pretzels and 3" stem to shamrock.

Fig. 1

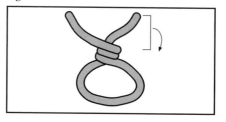

4. Measure around neck of jar; add 9". Cut a length of ribbon the determined measurement. Knot ribbon around neck of jar; notch ends. Glue shamrock to ribbon.

PICKLE PRETENDERS

*O*n April Fools' Day whip up a big batch of Dill Pickle Cracker Chips for pickle lovers! These crunchy "pickle pretenders" boast all the flavor of the real thing in a fun new package. Pack the snacks in a homestyle jar topped with a fabric-covered lid for a kosher presentation.

DILL PICKLE CRACKER CHIPS

- 2 packages (7½ ounces each) baked potato snack crackers
- ¼ cup vegetable oil
- 3 tablespoons white vinegar
- 2 tablespoons chopped fresh dill weed
- 1 tablespoon dry kosher dill pickle mix (in canning section)

Preheat oven to 200 degrees. Place crackers in a large roasting pan. In a small bowl, combine oil, vinegar, dill weed, and pickle mix. Stirring constantly, gradually drizzle mixture over crackers; stir to coat. Bake 40 minutes, stirring every 10 minutes. Spread on aluminum foil to cool. Store in an airtight container.

Yield: about 12 cups chips

"HOMEMADE PICKLES" JAR

You will need colored pencils, photocopy of label design (page 105), craft glue, tan card stock, decorative-edge craft scissors, black permanent fine-point marker, gallon jar with lid, fabric to cover lid, rubber band, jute twine, and a 1" dia. button.

Allow glue to dry after each application.

1. For label, use colored pencils to color design; cut out. Glue label to card stock. Leaving a ¼" border, use craft scissors to cut out label.
2. Use marker to draw "stitches" along edges of label; glue to front of jar.
3. Draw around jar lid on wrong side of fabric. Cut out 2" outside drawn line.

4. Place lid on jar and fabric over lid; secure with rubber band. Knot twine over rubber band. Thread ends of twine through button from back to front; tie ends together into a bow.

15

SPRING FLING

A spring-fresh delight, Lemon-Nut Balls are no-bake bites that boast zippy flavor. Rolled in confectioners sugar or coconut, the sweets are especially pleasing when served in a garden-inspired dish that's stamped with cheery motifs. The pretty posies will brighten anyone's day!

LEMON-NUT BALLS

  1 package (16 ounces) lemon-
      flavored confectioners sugar
  1 package (12 ounces) vanilla
      wafers, finely crushed
  1 cup chopped pecans, toasted and
      finely ground
  1/2 cup butter or margarine, melted
  1 can (6 ounces) frozen lemonade
      concentrate, thawed
      White confectioners sugar and
      flaked coconut

In a large bowl, combine lemon-flavored confectioners sugar, vanilla wafers, and pecans. Stir in melted butter and lemonade concentrate; mix until well combined. Shape mixture into 1-inch balls. Roll half of balls in white confectioners sugar and remaining balls in coconut. Store in an airtight container in refrigerator.

Yield: about 7 dozen balls

FLOWER-STAMPED CANDY DISH

For candy dish, you will need masking tape; a 5¼"w x 5¾"h clear octagonal candy dish with smooth sides and a 3¾"w base; yellow, metallic gold, red, aqua, green, dark green, and brown Delta CeramDecor™ Air-Dry Perm Enamel™ paint, surface conditioner, retarder, and clear gloss glaze; and ¼"w and liner paintbrushes.

For stamps, you will *also* need tracing paper, transfer paper, five 2" squares and five ½" x 2" pieces of balsa wood, craft foam, craft knife, cutting mat, and a hot glue gun.

For tag, you will *also* need craft glue, a 2⅜" x 3¾" piece of fabric, white poster board, black permanent fine-point marker, hole punch, 12" each of light green and pink satin ribbon, and 12" of gold cord.

Refer to Painting Techniques, page 122, for painting tips. Follow manufacturer's instructions to apply conditioner, paint, retarder, and glaze.

1. Placing bottom edge of tape ¼" below rim of dish, apply one strip of masking tape around top edge of dish. Leaving a ⅛" space between strips of tape, apply a second strip of masking tape around dish. Paint area between tape strips aqua, allow to dry and remove tape. Use aqua paint to paint a ¼" border around edge of base.
2. Use ¼"w paintbrush and gold paint to paint stripes on rim of dish and along border of base.

3. Use liner paintbrush to paint gold dots on aqua line around dish and around base.
4. For stamps, trace patterns, page 105, onto tracing paper. Use transfer paper to transfer one each of tulip, tulip leaf, stem, sunflower petals, sunflower leaves, and sunflower center to balsa wood squares (for placement only) and craft foam. Cut each shape from craft foam; glue to wood squares. Cutting close along outer edges of foam shapes, use craft knife to trim wood around foam. For handle, glue one short edge of one ½" x 2" wood piece perpendicular to back of each stamp.
5. Using paintbrush to apply paint to stamps and stamping on outside of dish only, stamp tulips red; tulip leaf, stem, and sunflower leaves green; sunflower petals yellow; and sunflower centers brown.
6. Use liner paintbrush to paint yellow dots on sunflower centers and for each tulip center; freehand green sunflower stems and veins on each leaf; paint dark green dots along edges of tulip leaves, stems, and along center vein on each sunflower leaf; and red detail lines on each sunflower petal.
7. For tag, glue fabric to poster board. Leaving ⅛" white border, cut out tag. Cut a 1¼" x 2" piece from poster board; glue to fabric-covered poster board. Use marker to write message on tag. Punch hole in corner of tag. Thread ribbons and cord through hole in tag. Knot cord ends.
8. Hand wash dish after each use.

WELCOME HOME, BABY!

*T*his thoughtful gift will bring warmth and comfort to Mommy and her wee one as they arrive home for the first time! Creamy Chicken Corn Chowder is a nutritiously filling meal for the new mother. Wrap a jar of the soup in a receiving blanket and top it off with a cute toy for baby to enjoy, too.

CREAMY CHICKEN CORN CHOWDER

- 3 pounds bone-in split chicken breasts
- 5 cups water
- 1 cup chopped onion
- 1 cup chopped celery
- 2 teaspoons salt
- 1/2 teaspoon ground black pepper
- 4 cups peeled, diced potatoes
- 1 cup thinly sliced carrots
- 1 can (14³/₄ ounces) cream-style corn
- 1 can (11 ounces) whole kernel corn, drained
- 1 jar (2 ounces) diced pimiento, drained
- 1 cup half and half

In a large stockpot, combine chicken, water, onion, celery, salt, and pepper. Cook over high heat until mixture boils. Cover and reduce heat to medium low; simmer about 1 hour or until chicken is tender. Remove chicken. Add potatoes and carrots to broth. Bring to a boil over high heat. Cover and reduce heat to medium low. Simmer 10 minutes or until vegetables are tender. While vegetables are cooking, skin and bone chicken; cut

into bite-size pieces. Stir chicken, corn, pimiento, and half and half into vegetable mixture. Cook 5 minutes or until heated through. Serve warm. Store in an airtight container in refrigerator.

Yield: about 14 cups chowder

NEW BABY GIFT

You will need a 5" dia. x 10³/₄"h jar with lid, receiving blanket, rubber band, 2¹/₂ yds. of sheer wired ribbon, craft wire, wire cutters, safety pin, and a stuffed toy. *For tag,* you will *also* need decorative-edge scissors, card stock, black permanent fine-point marker, and a diaper pin.

1. Place gift in jar. Gather blanket around jar; secure with rubber band. Cut a 28" length from ribbon; knot around rubber band. Notch ribbon ends.

2. Using remaining ribbon, follow *Making a Bow*, page 121, to make a bow with six 8" loops and two 2" streamers. Use wire ends to attach bow around gathers. Pin toy to center of bow.

3. For tag, use craft scissors to cut a 2¹/₄" square from card stock. Use marker to write message on tag. Use diaper pin to pin tag to blanket.

HIPPITY-HOPPITY TOFFEE

*O*ur Pastel Easter Toffee *is a hippity-hoppity treat! The buttery bits are drizzled with tinted candy coating for a marbleized effect. Nestle the candy inside a papier-mâché egg decorated with buttons and rickrack.*

PASTEL EASTER TOFFEE

- ³/₄ cup butter
- 1 cup sugar
- ¹/₃ cup water
- 1 tablespoon light corn syrup
- 1 teaspoon vanilla extract
- 12 ounces vanilla candy coating, chopped
- ¹/₂ teaspoon vegetable shortening
  Blue, green, pink, and yellow paste food colors

Line a 9 x 13-inch baking pan with aluminum foil, extending foil over ends of pan; grease foil. Butter sides of a very heavy large saucepan. Combine butter, sugar, water, and corn syrup in saucepan. Stirring constantly, cook over medium-low heat until sugar dissolves. Using a pastry brush dipped in hot water, wash down any sugar crystals on sides of pan. Attach a candy thermometer to pan, making sure thermometer does not touch bottom of pan. Increase heat to medium and bring to a boil. Cook, without stirring, until mixture reaches soft-crack stage (approximately 270 to 290 degrees). Test about ¹/₂ teaspoon mixture in ice water. Mixture will form hard threads in ice water but will soften when removed from water. Remove from heat and stir in vanilla. Spread mixture into prepared pan.

Place candy coating and shortening in a medium microwave-safe bowl. Microwave on medium-high power (80%) 3 minutes or until coating melts, stirring after each minute. Place 1 tablespoon melted coating into each of 4 bowls. Tint coating blue, green, pink, and yellow. Spread remaining coating over warm toffee. Working quickly before untinted coating hardens, drizzle tinted coatings over toffee (reheating tinted coatings as necessary). Use a table knife to swirl colors through coating. Gently tap pan on counter to smooth candy surface. Let candy cool.

Use ends of foil to lift toffee from pan; break into pieces. Store in an airtight container.

Yield: about 1 pound, 7 ounces candy

DECORATED EGG

You will need acrylic paint, paintbrush, papier-mâché egg-shaped box (we used an 8¹/₂"h box), hot glue gun, assorted buttons, assorted rickrack, and shredded paper.

Throughout these instructions, we refer to the egg box as "egg."

1. Remove lid from egg. Paint entire egg; allow to dry.
2. Glue buttons and rickrack to egg as desired.
3. Line inside bottom of egg with shredded paper; place gift in egg. Place lid on egg.

NO-BAKE BUNNY TREAT

*H*ere comes the Easter Bunny to deliver a sweet surprise to someone dear! This simple no-bake cheesecake is decorated with jelly bean "eggs" and tinted coconut "Easter grass." Friends will be delighted to find the yummy dessert inside a cute fabric-covered box sporting a craft foam bunny face.

NO-BAKE WHITE CHOCOLATE CHEESECAKE

  1 package (11.1 ounces) no-bake cheesecake mix

CRUST

  2 tablespoons sugar

  $^1/_3$ cup sliced almonds, toasted and finely ground

  $^1/_3$ cup butter or margarine, melted

FILLING

  $1^1/_3$ cups milk

  2 teaspoons vanilla extract

  $^1/_2$ teaspoon ground cinnamon

TOPPING

  $^1/_4$ cup whipping cream

  1 package (6 ounces) white baking chocolate, chopped

  $1^1/_2$ cups flaked coconut

  $1^1/_2$ teaspoons water

  3 drops green liquid food coloring

    Assorted colors of small gourmet jelly beans

For crust, combine graham cracker crust envelope from cheesecake mix, sugar, almonds, and melted butter in a small bowl. Press into bottom of a lightly greased 9-inch springform pan.

For filling, combine filling envelope from cheesecake mix, milk, vanilla, and cinnamon in a medium bowl. Mix according to package directions. Pour into crust. Cover and chill 30 minutes.

For topping, combine whipping cream and white chocolate in a small bowl. Microwave on medium power (50%) 2 minutes or until chocolate softens, stirring after each minute. Spread over filling. Cover and chill 30 minutes or until topping is set. Combine coconut, water, and green food coloring in a resealable plastic bag; shake until coconut is tinted. Decorate cake with coconut and jelly beans. Store in an airtight container in refrigerator.

Yield: about 8 servings

EASTER BUNNY CAKE BOX

You will need a 10" square x 4"d cake box, wrapping paper, spray adhesive, craft knife and cutting mat, tracing paper, white and pink craft foam, transfer paper, black permanent marker, low temperature glue gun, $^5/_8$" dia. pink button, and 22" of $1^1/_2$"w ribbon.

Use low temperature glue gun for all gluing unless otherwise indicated.

1. Unfold box. Cut a piece of wrapping paper 1" larger on all sides than unfolded box. Place wrapping paper wrong side up on a flat surface.
2. Apply spray adhesive to outside of entire box. Center unfolded box adhesive side down on paper; press firmly to secure.
3. Use craft knife to cut paper even with edges of box. If box has slits, use craft knife to cut through slits from inside of box; reassemble box.
4. Trace patterns, page 106, onto tracing paper. Use patterns to cut one head and two ears from white foam and two inner ears from pink foam. Use transfer paper to transfer face details to head.
5. Use marker to draw over transferred lines and to color pupils of eyes.
6. Glue inner ears to ears and button to face for nose.
7. Tie ribbon into bow; trim ends. Arrange and glue ears, head, and bow on box.

FOR A "SOUP-ER" SECRETARY

*O*n Secretaries Day, remember a top-notch assistant with this busy-day lunch basket. Tuck in a jar of our soothing soup that mixes up in just minutes — simply add milk and pop it in the microwave. To complete the kit, include some crackers and pretty tableware for a special "type" of lunch!

BUSY DAY POTATO SOUP MIX

  1 package (6.6 ounces) dried potato flakes
  2 tablespoons dried minced onions
  2 tablespoons chicken bouillon granules
  2 teaspoons celery salt
  2 teaspoons dried parsley flakes
  2 teaspoons dried chopped chives
$1/2$ teaspoon garlic powder
$1/2$ teaspoon salt
$1/4$ teaspoon ground black pepper
$1/8$ teaspoon ground red pepper

In a medium bowl, combine potato flakes, minced onions, bouillon, celery salt, parsley flakes, chopped chives, garlic powder, salt, black pepper, and red pepper. Store in an airtight container. Give with serving instructions.

Yield: about 4 cups soup mix

To serve: In a 2-cup microwave-safe container, combine $1/3$ cup soup mix with 1 cup milk. Microwave on high power (100%) 3 minutes or until soup is thick and smooth and onions are tender, stirring after each minute.

Yield: about 1 cup soup

SECRETARIES DAY TAG

You will need white and colored card stock, craft glue, decorative-edge craft scissors, black permanent fine-point marker, hole punch, and 6" of $1/8$"w satin ribbon.

1. Cut a $1 5/8$" x 3" piece of white card stock; glue to colored card stock; allow to dry. Leaving a $3/8$" colored border, use craft scissors to cut out tag. Use marker to write message on tag and to draw "stitches" along outside edges of white card stock.

2. Punch hole in tag. Use ribbon to attach tag to basket.

EARTH OR BUST!

A celebration for youngsters just isn't complete without clever party favors filled with crunchy snacks! An orange-flavored candy coating – made using gelatin and soft-drink mix – transforms ordinary peanuts into fun-to-munch "moon rocks." For a real blast, pack them in paper towel-tube "rockets" decorated with poster board and paint in neon colors.

ORANGE "MOON ROCKS" PEANUTS

- 2 egg whites
- 1/2 cup sugar
- 1 package (3 ounces) orange gelatin
- 1 package (0.15 ounce) orange-flavored soft drink mix
- 1 container (12 ounces) dry-roasted peanuts

Preheat oven to 225 degrees. In a medium bowl, beat egg whites until foamy. Gradually adding sugar, gelatin, and soft drink mix, beat until soft peaks form. Stir in peanuts. Spread in a single layer on a greased 10¹/₂ x 15¹/₂-inch jellyroll pan. Bake 1 hour, stirring every 15 minutes. Cool completely on pan. Store in an airtight container.

Yield: about 5¹/₂ cups peanuts

ROCKET PARTY FAVORS

For each rocket, you will need decorative-edge craft scissors, card stock to cover tube (we used blue or grey), 5¹/₄" of cardboard tube from paper towel roll, star-shaped rubber stamp, gold ink pad, white and silver paint pens, hot glue

gun, neon-colored dimensional paint, tracing paper, neon-colored poster boards, and clear tape.

1. Using craft scissors, cut a 5¹/₂" x 6" piece from card stock.
2. Stamp gold stars on card stock. Use paint pens and dimensional paint to paint designs and message on card stock.
3. For rocket, overlapping ends and matching top edges, glue card stock around tube. Spacing evenly, cut four 1" slits around bottom of rocket.
4. Trace patterns, page 107, onto tracing paper; cut out. Use patterns to cut a half-circle and two fins from poster board.
5. Mark center of each fin. Beginning at top and leaving ¹/₂" uncut, cut a slit in center of one fin. Beginning at bottom, repeat to cut slit in remaining fin. Slide fin pieces together; tape to secure. Slide slits in rocket over fins.
6. Use craft scissors to trim curved edge of half circle. Overlapping straight edges, form into a cone shape; tape to secure.
7. Place gift in rocket; glue cone to top of rocket.

23

*M*ake Mother's Day extra special – fill a rose-trimmed candy box with delicate chocolate-covered candies flavored with a hint of rose water. The tiny icing flowers on each piece coordinate perfectly with the wreath of dried rosebuds that crowns the box.

MOTHER'S DAY CANDIES

CANDIES

- 1 cup sugar
- 1 cup light corn syrup
- ²/₃ cup water
- 1 package (1³/₄ ounces) powdered fruit pectin
- ¹/₂ teaspoon baking soda
- 3 tablespoons rose water (available at gourmet food stores)
- 1 drop red liquid food coloring
- 8 ounces chocolate candy coating, chopped
- 4 ounces bittersweet baking chocolate, chopped

DECORATING ICING

- 1 cup confectioners sugar
- 2 tablespoons vegetable shortening
- 2 to 3 teaspoons rose water
   Burgundy and green paste food coloring

For candies, line a 5 x 9-inch loaf pan with aluminum foil, extending foil over ends of pan; grease foil. Butter sides of a heavy medium saucepan. Combine sugar and corn syrup. Stirring constantly, cook over medium-low heat until sugar dissolves. Using a pastry brush dipped in hot water, wash down any sugar crystals on sides of pan. Attach a candy

thermometer to pan, making sure thermometer does not touch bottom of pan. Increase heat to medium-high and bring to a boil. While cooking sugar mixture, combine water, pectin, and baking soda in another medium saucepan. Stirring frequently, cook pectin mixture over high heat until mixture boils. Remove from heat. Cook sugar mixture, stirring occasionally, until mixture reaches soft-crack stage (approximately 270 to 290 degrees). Test about ¹/₂ teaspoon mixture in ice water. Mixture will form hard threads in ice water but will soften when removed from water. Bring pectin mixture back to a boil. Stirring constantly, slowly pour sugar mixture into boiling pectin mixture; cook 2 minutes. Remove from heat. Stir in rose water and food coloring. Pour mixture into prepared pan. Allow mixture to cool 2 hours at room temperature or until firm.

Use ends of foil to lift candy from pan. Use an oiled knife to cut into ³/₄-inch by 1-inch pieces. In a heavy medium saucepan over low heat, melt candy coating and chocolate. Remove chocolate from heat (if chocolate begins to harden, return to heat). Placing each jelly candy on a fork and holding over saucepan, spoon chocolate over candy. Place candies on a baking sheet lined with waxed paper; chill 10 minutes or until chocolate hardens.

For decorating icing, combine confectioners sugar, shortening, and rose water in a small bowl; beat until smooth. Transfer icing into 2 small bowls; tint burgundy and green. Spoon burgundy icing into a pastry bag fitted with a small petal tip. Pipe rosebuds onto candies. Spoon green icing into a pastry bag fitted with a small round tip. Pipe stems onto rosebuds. Let icing harden. Store candies in a single layer in an airtight container in refrigerator.

Yield: about 4 dozen candies

MOTHER'S DAY CANDY BOX

You will need an 11" dia. x 1³/₄"h round papier-mâché box, antique white spray paint, hot glue gun, ³/₈"w gold gimp trim, ¹/₄"w pink rose trim, 2 yds. of 2"w pink sheer ribbon, 6¹/₂"w heart-shaped dried rosebud wreath, "Mother" charm, and a purchased 2" x 4" gift tag.

1. Paint box antique white; allow to dry.
2. Trimming to fit, glue trims along edge on top of lid.
3. Place gift in box. Wrap ribbon around box and through wreath. Tie ribbon into a double bow; notch ends. Glue charm to knot of bow.
4. Write message on tag; insert under ribbon.

WORLD'S BEST MOM

*S*how *Mom you think the world of her with a gift of easy Cappuccino Coffee Creamer tucked in a sweet cross-stitched mug. The cup is a lasting reminder of your love that will make relaxing for a "coffee break" especially nice.*

CAPPUCCINO COFFEE CREAMER

  1 jar (8 ounces) non-dairy powdered
       coffee creamer
$3/4$ teaspoon ground cinnamon
$1/2$ teaspoon orange extract

Process creamer and cinnamon in a small food processor until blended. Sprinkle orange extract over creamer mixture; process until well blended. Store in an airtight container in a cool place. Give with serving instructions.

Yield: about $2^{1}/4$ cups creamer

To serve: Add creamer to hot coffee; stir until blended. Serve hot or iced.

GIFT BAG AND MUG

For mug, you will need embroidery floss (see color key, page 107), white Stitch-A-Mug™ with a white Vinyl-Weave™ insert (14 ct), plastic bag to fit in mug, and 8" of $1/4$"w white grosgrain ribbon.
For bag, you will need a hot glue gun, $3^{1}/4$"w wooden puffed heart (painted pink), decorative bag with handles (we used a 5" x $8^{1}/4$" bag), 24" of $7/8$"w ribbon, and tissue paper.

Refer to Cross Stitch, page 123, before beginning project.

1. Using three strands of floss for *Cross Stitch* and one strand for *Backstitch,*

follow manufacturer's instructions to center and stitch design, page 107, on Vinyl-Weave™.
2. Follow manufacturer's instructions to insert stitched piece into Stitch-A-Mug™.

3. Place plastic bag in mug; fill bag with creamer. Knot grosgrain ribbon around top of bag.
4. Glue heart to bag. Tie ribbon into a bow around handle. Line bag with tissue paper. Place mug in bag.

JUST FOR YOU!

Treat a friend who's been especially sweet with luscious Blackberry Swirl Cheesecake. Its elegant marbled look is formed by drawing a knife through the blackberry jam topping. Create a beribboned gift tag using craft foam, paint markers, and sprigs of faux berries.

BLACKBERRY SWIRL CHEESECAKE

- 1/2 cup seedless blackberry jam
- 4 packages (8 ounces each) cream cheese, softened
- 1 cup sugar
- 4 eggs
- 2 tablespoons freshly squeezed lemon juice
- 1 tablespoon vanilla extract

Preheat oven to 350 degrees. In a small saucepan, melt jam over low heat; set aside. Wrap aluminum foil under and around outside of a 9-inch springform pan. In a large bowl, beat cream cheese and sugar until fluffy. Add eggs, 1 at a time, beating well after each addition. Beat in lemon juice and vanilla. Pour 2 cups batter into prepared pan. Drizzle 3 tablespoons jam over batter. Repeat layers 2 more times, ending with 2 tablespoons jam on top. Use a knife to swirl jam through batter. Place springform pan in a larger baking pan. Pour hot water into larger pan to a depth of 1/2 inch. Bake 1 hour or until top is lightly browned and cheesecake is firm around edges. Remove springform pan from water. Cool completely on a wire rack.

Cover and chill 2 hours before serving. Remove sides of pan. Serve chilled.

Yield: about 16 servings

BLACKBERRY GIFT TAG

You will need a drawing compass; black craft foam; decorative-edge craft scissors; red, green, and neon-green fine-point paint pens; hole punch; 14" of 1 1/2"w wired ribbon; 8" of 1/8"w satin ribbon; artificial floral pick with berries; and a low temperature glue gun.

1. For blackberry, use compass to draw a 3 1/2" dia. circle on craft foam. Use craft scissors to cut out blackberry.
2. Use green paint pen to write message on blackberry; add neon-green highlights. Use red paint pen to paint details on blackberry. Punch hole at top of blackberry.
3. Tie wired ribbon into a bow; notch ribbon ends.
4. Use satin ribbon to attach blackberry to bow. Insert floral pick into knot of bow; glue to secure.

WAKE-UP CALL

When you have house guests, treat them to a continental breakfast. Piped full of cherry jelly, our homemade Jelly-Filled Doughnuts are sprinkled with confectioners sugar and served in a charming picket fence basket. A faux bird nest and beribboned spray add a cheerful greeting to start the day.

JELLY-FILLED DOUGHNUTS

2   packages dry yeast
$^{1}/_{2}$ cup warm milk
6   tablespoons granulated sugar
$^{1}/_{4}$ cup vegetable shortening
1   teaspoon baking powder
$^{1}/_{2}$ teaspoon salt
$^{1}/_{2}$ cup hot water
1   egg
3   to 3$^{1}/_{2}$ cups all-purpose flour
    Vegetable cooking spray
    Vegetable oil
1   cup cherry jelly
    Confectioners sugar

In a small bowl, dissolve yeast in warm milk. In a large bowl, combine granulated sugar, shortening, baking powder, and salt. Add hot water; beat with an electric mixer until shortening is almost melted. Add yeast mixture and egg; beat until blended. Add 3 cups flour; stir until a soft dough forms. Turn onto a lightly floured surface and knead about 5 minutes or until dough becomes smooth and elastic, using additional flour as necessary. Place in a large bowl sprayed with cooking spray, turning once to coat top of dough. Cover and let rise in a warm place (80 to 85 degrees) 1 hour or until doubled in size.

Turn dough onto a lightly floured surface and punch down. Use a floured rolling pin to roll out dough to $^{1}/_{2}$-inch thickness. Use a 2$^{3}/_{4}$-inch-diameter biscuit cutter to cut out doughnuts. Place 1$^{1}/_{2}$ inches apart on a greased baking sheet. Lightly spray tops of doughnuts with cooking spray, cover, and let rise in a warm place 45 minutes or until doubled in size.

Heat oil in a large saucepan to about 360 degrees. Deep fry doughnuts in hot oil until golden brown, turning once. Drain on paper towels and cool.

To fill doughnuts, cut a small slit in side of each doughnut. Transfer jelly to a pastry bag fitted with a large round tip. Pipe jelly into doughnuts. Sift confectioners sugar over doughnuts. Serve warm.

Yield: about 1$^{1}/_{2}$ dozen doughnuts

PICKET FENCE BASKET

You will need 2 yds. of 1$^{1}/_{2}$"w wired ribbon; craft wire; wire cutters; hot glue gun; 3" dia. artificial nest with bird and eggs; artificial greenery, berries, and small flowers; fabric to line basket, and a 10" square white picket fence-style basket with handle.

For tag, you will *also* need white and blue card stock, brown permanent fine-point marker, decorative-edge craft scissors, and craft glue.

Use hot glue for all gluing unless otherwise indicated.

1. Follow *Making a Bow,* page 121, to make a bow with seven 6" loops and two 11" streamers.
2. Glue eggs and bird to nest. Arrange and glue bow, greenery, berries, and flowers to handle. Glue nest to bow.
3. Arrange fabric in basket.
4. For tag, cut a 1$^{1}/_{4}$" x 2$^{1}/_{2}$" piece from white card stock. Use marker to write message on tag. Use craft scissors to trim short ends. Use craft glue to glue tag to blue card stock. Leaving a $^{1}/_{8}$" blue border, cut out tag. Glue tag to bow.

EXTRA easy!

*T*o teach is to love, and any teacher is sure to love these delicious Curried Cheese Snacks! A touch of curry powder adds zing to the crunchy mix, which can be made in minutes. Embellish gift bags with clever ruler bookmarks to create perfect teacher gifts for any occasion.

CURRIED CHEESE SNACKS

- 1 package (10 ounces) cheese snack crackers
- 1 package (7$\frac{1}{2}$ ounces) baked pretzel crackers
- 3 cups square corn cereal
- 3 cups square rice cereal
- 1 cup dry-roasted peanuts
- $\frac{3}{4}$ cup butter or margarine, melted
- 2 envelopes (1$\frac{1}{4}$ ounces each) cheese sauce mix
- 2 teaspoons curry powder

Preheat oven to 350 degrees. Combine crackers, cereal, and peanuts in a large roasting pan. In a small bowl, combine melted butter, sauce mix, and curry powder; stir until blended. Pour over cracker mixture; stir until well coated. Bake 15 minutes or until lightly browned, stirring every 5 minutes. Spread on aluminum foil to cool. Store in an airtight container.

Yield: about 19 cups cheese snacks

"TEACHERS RULE" GIFT BAGS

For each bag, you will need a gift bag with handles (we used a 5" x 8$\frac{1}{4}$" bag), $\frac{5}{8}$"w gingham ribbon, and craft glue.

For each bookmark, you will *also* need a 1$\frac{3}{8}$" x 10$\frac{1}{2}$" piece of poster board; 10$\frac{1}{2}$" length each of $\frac{5}{8}$"w ruler-motif ribbon and 1$\frac{3}{8}$"w gingham ribbon; tracing paper; red, green, and brown felt; gold self-adhesive star sticker; and double-sided tape.

For each tag, you will *also* need two colors of card stock, black permanent medium-point marker, and gold self-adhesive star stickers.

Allow glue to dry after each application.

1. Measure across front of bag. Cut a length of $\frac{5}{8}$"w gingham ribbon the determined measurement; glue to front of bag.

2. For bookmark, glue 1$\frac{3}{8}$"w ribbon, then ruler-motif ribbon to poster board.

3. Trace patterns, page 108, onto tracing paper. Using patterns, cut apple from red felt, stem from brown felt, and leaves from green felt. Overlapping as necessary, glue shapes together. Apply star to apple. Glue apple to top of bookmark.

4. For tag, cut a 2" x 4" piece from one color of card stock. Use marker to write message and to draw design along top and bottom of tag. Glue tag to remaining card stock. Leaving a $\frac{1}{4}$" border, cut out tag. Apply stars to tag. Tape tag and bookmark to front of bag.

BAYOU BAGEL CHIPS

*L*et the good times roll with a batch of our spicy Cajun Bagel Chips. The crispy bites feature Louisiana-style flavors such as onion, garlic, and red pepper for snacks with real bite! Seal them in an airtight container and top it off with a fun alligator-shaped tag.

CAJUN BAGEL CHIPS

Chill bagels at least 1 hour for easier slicing.

- 6 plain bagels
- 6 tablespoons butter or margarine, softened
- 1 teaspoon dried parsley flakes
- 1 teaspoon dried minced onion
- 1 teaspoon garlic powder
- 1/2 teaspoon ground red pepper
- 1/2 teaspoon salt
- 1/4 teaspoon ground black pepper

To slice each bagel, place bagel flat on cutting board. With a serrated knife, cut bagel in half vertically. Place halves on cutting board, cut side down. Cut halves into about 1/4-inch slices.

Preheat oven to 325 degrees. In a small bowl, combine butter, parsley, onion, garlic powder, red pepper, salt, and black pepper; beat until well blended. Spread about 1/4 teaspoon butter mixture over 1 side of each bagel slice. Place slices, buttered side up, on ungreased baking sheets. Bake 15 to 20 minutes or until lightly browned. Cool on a wire rack. Store in an airtight container.

Yield: about 14 cups bagel chips

ALLIGATOR GIFT TOPPER

You will need tracing paper, transfer paper, green card stock, black permanent fine-point marker, container with lid (we used a 4 1/4" dia. x 8 1/4"h canister with a window), 1 5/8"w wired ribbon, craft wire, wire cutters, hot glue gun, and a red pepper floral pick.

1. Trace alligator tag pattern, page 108, onto tracing paper. Use transfer paper to transfer design to card stock. Use marker to draw over all transferred lines and to write message on tag. Leaving a 1/8" border, cut out tag.

2. Place gift in container; replace lid. Knot a length of ribbon around container. Use remaining ribbon and follow *Making a Bow,* page 121, to make a bow with four desired size loops and two streamers. Wire bow to knot of ribbon. Glue pick and tag to bow.

MAPLE MORNING TREAT

*A*n eye-opening variation of a traditional favorite, Maple-Cinnamon French Toast offers a yummy way to greet the day. To deliver a ready-to-bake breakfast, wrap the pan with a bright napkin and add the baking instructions.

MAPLE-CINNAMON FRENCH TOAST

Assemble French toast the day before baking to let flavors blend.

- 12 cups 1-inch cubes of French bread (about one 16-ounce loaf)
- 1/2 cup golden raisins
- 1 package (8 ounces) cream cheese, softened
- 2 cups whipping cream
- 1/2 cup maple syrup
- 12 eggs
- 1 teaspoon vanilla extract
- 1/2 teaspoon ground cinnamon
- 1/8 teaspoon salt

Divide bread cubes evenly into 2 greased 8³/₈ x 12³/₈ x 1¹/₈-inch aluminum foil baking pans with plastic lids. Sprinkle raisins evenly over bread. In a large bowl, beat cream cheese until fluffy. Gradually beat in whipping cream and maple syrup; beat until well combined. Beat in eggs, vanilla, cinnamon, and salt. Pour mixture over bread, pressing bread into mixture, if necessary. Cover and chill 8 hours or overnight. Give with baking instructions.

Yield: about 6 servings in each pan

To bake: Allow pan to stand at room temperature 30 minutes. Remove plastic

lid and cover pan with aluminum foil. Bake in a 375-degree oven 25 minutes. Remove foil and bake 18 to 22 minutes longer or until center is set and top is golden brown. Serve warm with maple syrup.

WRAPPED PAN AND GIFT TAG

You will need a covered pan (from recipe, this page), 20" square cloth napkin, safety pins, 1 yd. of sheer wired ribbon, 3" dia. artificial flower, and a hot glue gun.

For tag, you will *also* need decorative-edge craft scissors, card stock, black permanent fine-point marker, hole punch, and 8" of ¹/₈"w satin ribbon.

1. Place covered pan diagonally at center on wrong side of napkin. Fold corners to top of pan cover; pin to secure. Tie ribbon into a bow around width of pan. Glue flower to knot of bow.
2. For tag, use craft scissors to cut a 2¹/₄" x 4" piece from card stock. Use marker to write baking instructions on tag. Punch hole in tag. Use satin ribbon to attach tag to bow.

SUMMERTIME SPARKLER

*W*hen the heat is
on, stir up a batch of Ginger
Limeade Sparkle and create
some summertime relief for
two! Fresh ginger lends a sweet,
peppery zing to the lime-flavored
concoction. Tuck a jug of the
refreshment in a basket along
with club soda and a pair of
stylish glasses for serving.

GINGER LIMEADE SPARKLE

    3 cups water
    2 cups sugar
    1 piece (4 ounces) gingerroot,
          peeled and sliced crosswise into
          4 pieces
    2 cans (12 ounces each) frozen
          limeade concentrate, thawed

In a medium saucepan, combine water,
sugar, and gingerroot. Stirring frequently,
bring to a boil over medium-high heat.
Reduce heat to medium-low and simmer
5 minutes. Remove from heat and let
stand 30 minutes.

Strain syrup into a 1-gallon container;
discard gingerroot. Stir in limeade. Cover
and store in refrigerator. Give with serving
instructions.

Yield: about 7 cups concentrate

To serve: Stir two 1-liter bottles club soda
into concentrate. Serve over ice. Garnish
with lime zest strips.

"Bee" Is For Bread

Give the goodness of oatmeal in a delicious home-baked bread! Topped with sweet honey butter, this hearty loaf is packed with natural energy. To perk up someone's day, embellish a purchased gift bag with sunny flowers and a natural raffia bow. An appliquéd dish towel will add an extra buzz.

HONEY-TOP OATMEAL BREAD

BREAD
- 1 package dry yeast
- 3/4 cup warm milk
- 6 tablespoons vegetable shortening
- 6 tablespoons sugar
- 3/4 teaspoon salt
- 1 cup hot water
- 1 3/4 cups old-fashioned oats
- 1 egg
- 4 to 4 1/2 cups all-purpose flour
  Vegetable cooking spray

HONEY BUTTER
- 1/2 cup butter, softened
- 1/3 cup honey

For bread, dissolve yeast in warm milk in a small bowl. In a large bowl, combine shortening, sugar, and salt. Add hot water; beat with an electric mixer until shortening is almost melted. Add oats, egg, and yeast mixture; beat until blended. Add 4 cups flour; stir until a soft dough forms. Turn onto a lightly floured surface and knead about 5 minutes or until dough becomes smooth and elastic, using additional flour as necessary. Place in a large bowl sprayed with cooking spray, turning once to coat top of dough. Cover and let rise in a warm place (80 to 85 degrees) 1 1/2 hours or until doubled in size.

Turn dough onto a lightly floured surface and punch down. Shape dough into 2 loaves and place in 2 greased 4 x 8-inch loaf pans. With a sharp knife, make a slit (about 1/2 inch deep) down center of each loaf. Spray tops of dough with cooking spray, cover, and let rise in a warm place 1 hour or until doubled in size.

For honey butter, combine butter and honey in a small bowl. Beat with an electric mixer until well blended; set aside.

Preheat oven to 350 degrees. Carefully spread 2 tablespoons honey butter mixture in slit on each loaf of bread. Bake 25 to 35 minutes or until bread is golden brown and sounds hollow when tapped. Serve warm or transfer to a wire rack to cool completely. Store in an airtight container. Give with remaining honey butter.

Yield: 2 loaves bread and about 3/4 cup honey butter

HONEY BEE GIFT ENSEMBLE

HONEY BEE TOWEL
You will need paper-backed fusible web, fabric scraps, dish towel, and embroidery floss.

Refer to Embroidery Stitches, page 123, and use three strands of floss for all stitching.

1. Use patterns, page 108, and follow *Making Appliqués*, page 122, to make one hive, three body, and six wing appliqués from fabric scraps.
2. Arrange appliqués on towel; fuse in place.

3. Work *Stem Stitch* to outline bees and layers of hive. Work *Running Stitch* for bee trails. Work a *Cross Stitch* across center of each wingspan.

HONEY BEE GIFT BAG
You will need a corrugated cardboard gift bag with handles (we used an 8 1/2" x 10" bag), 12" of floral wire, silk flowers and greenery (we used twigs, ivy leaves, and assorted grasses), hot glue gun, and raffia.

1. Wrap wire around stems of flowers, twigs, and greenery; twist in back to secure. Glue to front of bag. Cut several 15" lengths of raffia; tie into a bow. Glue bow to stems, covering wire.

GIFT TAG
You will need tracing paper, transfer paper, 1 3/4" x 2 3/4" piece of cream-colored paper, craft glue, black fine-point permanent marker, yellow card stock, decorative-edge craft scissors, hole punch, and an artificial bee.

1. Trace pattern, page 108, onto tracing paper. Use transfer paper to transfer tag design to cream-colored paper. Use marker to draw "stitches" along edges of tag. Glue to yellow card stock. Leaving a 1/4" yellow border, use craft scissors to cut out tag.
2. Punch hole in tag. Use a strand of raffia to attach tag to gift. Glue bee to tag.

"BERRY" ZESTY GIFT

A *blend of sweet and savory flavors, our Strawberry-Mint Vinaigrette is a fresh, zesty dressing for a crisp salad. Top the jar with cross-stitched berries and present it in a basket along with a matching fingertip towel. It'll be a "berry" special offering!*

STRAWBERRY-MINT VINAIGRETTE

- 1 jar (18 ounces) strawberry preserves
- 1/4 cup freshly squeezed lemon juice
- 2 tablespoons vegetable oil
- 2 tablespoons red wine vinegar
- 2 tablespoons chopped fresh mint leaves
- 1 teaspoon finely chopped onion
- 1/2 teaspoon grated lemon zest
- 1/4 teaspoon salt
- 1/4 teaspoon ground black pepper

Process preserves, lemon juice, oil, vinegar, mint, onion, lemon zest, salt, and pepper in a food processor until smooth. Pour into jars with lids. Let stand at room temperature 2 hours for flavors to blend. Store in refrigerator. Serve at room temperature.

Yield: about 2 cups vinaigrette

STRAWBERRY GIFT COLLECTION

Refer to Cross Stitch, page 123, before beginning projects. Use three strands of floss for Cross Stitch and one strand for Backstitch.

BASKET
You will need a basket with handle (we used a 7" dia. red basket), natural wood excelsior, 1¼" x 12" torn fabric strip, hot glue gun, and a silk daisy.

1. Line basket with excelsior. Tie fabric strip into a bow around handle.
2. Glue daisy to knot of bow.

TOWEL
You will need embroidery floss (see color key, page 109) and a fingertip towel with 2½"w border of Aida (14 ct).

1. Center and stitch towel design, page 109, on border.
2. Place towel in basket.

JAR LID
You will need embroidery floss (see color key, page 109), 6" square of Ivory Aida (14 ct), wide-mouth canning jar with lid, cardboard, batting, craft glue, and raffia.

1. Center and stitch jar lid design, page 109, on Aida.
2. For jar lid insert, use flat part of jar lid as a pattern and cut one circle each from cardboard, batting, and stitched piece. Glue batting circle to cardboard circle. Center stitched piece right side up on batting; glue edges of stitched piece to batting; allow to dry.
3. Before presenting gift, remove band from filled jar; place insert in band and replace band over lid. Knot raffia around band.

THANKFUL SPIRITS

EXTRA easy!

*O*ffer a bounty of thanks
with a spirited gift of Minted Wine.
It's so easy to add zip to purchased
white wine by flavoring it with
fresh mint leaves! Deliver a bottle
in an elegant leaf-stamped bag.

MINTED WINE

  1 bottle (750 ml) white wine
  1 tablespoon chopped fresh mint

In a 2-quart container, combine wine
and mint. Cover and chill 24 hours. Strain
wine mixture into gift bottle. Store in
refrigerator; serve chilled.

Yield: about $3^1/_3$ cups wine

LEAF PRINT BOTTLE BAG

You will need green acrylic paint,
paintbrush, fresh mint leaves in assorted
sizes, $7^1/_2$" x 15" canvas bag, gold
dimensional paint, 26" of $1^1/_2$"w wired
ribbon, and a 7" berry sprig.
For tag, you will *also* need card stock
and a permanent medium-point marker.

*Allow paint to dry after each
application.*

1. For each leaf design, use paintbrush to
apply paint to one side of leaf. Using leaf
as a stamp, press prints of leaves on bag.
2. Use dimensional paint to outline
stamped leaves, draw over center veins,
and add dots at base of several leaves.
3. Place gift in bag. Tie ribbon into a
bow around bag. Insert berry sprig
under ribbon.
4. For tag, cut a 3" x $4^1/_4$" piece from
card stock. Matching short edges, fold
tag in half. Use marker to write message
on tag.

"TURNOVER" A NEW DAY

*H*elp *a hurried friend start the day with a quick, hearty breakfast — deliver a basketful of frozen Sausage Breakfast Turnovers! The savory bites are ready to pop straight from the freezer into the oven. Wrap them in a colorful kitchen towel and deliver with baking instructions.*

SAUSAGE BREAKFAST TURNOVERS

    1   package (16 ounces) bulk pork
          sausage
  1/3   cup chopped onion
  1/3   cup chopped green pepper
    3   cans (12 ounces, 10 count each)
          refrigerated biscuits
    1   cup (4 ounces) finely shredded
          Cheddar cheese
    1   egg white, beaten

In a large skillet, cook sausage over medium heat until lightly browned. Add onion and pepper; cook until vegetables are tender. Transfer sausage mixture to a colander to drain; cool.

On a lightly floured surface, use a floured rolling pin to roll each biscuit into a 4-inch circle. In a medium bowl, combine sausage mixture and cheese. Spoon 1 tablespoon sausage mixture on half of each biscuit, leaving edges free. Brush egg white on edges. Fold biscuits in half; press edges with a fork. Prick tops of turnovers with fork. Transfer turnovers to a baking sheet. Place in freezer 1 hour or until firm. Transfer to a resealable plastic bag; store in freezer. Give with baking instructions.

Yield: 30 turnovers

To bake: Place frozen turnovers on an ungreased baking sheet. Let stand at room temperature 30 minutes. Bake in a 350-degree oven 13 to 16 minutes or until heated through and golden brown. Serve warm.

RISE AND SHINE BASKET

You will need tracing paper, decorative-edge craft scissors, white and yellow card stock, transfer paper, black permanent fine-point marker, pink and blue highlighters, craft glue, 1/8" dia. hole punch, basket (we used an 8" x 11" oval basket), dish towel, rubber band, 1"w and assorted ribbons to coordinate with towel, and 12" of 1/16"w satin ribbon.

1. Trace sun and cloud patterns, page 109, onto tracing paper; cut out.

Using patterns, cut cloud from white card stock and use decorative-edge craft scissors to cut sun from yellow card stock. Use transfer paper to transfer detail lines to shapes.
2. Use black marker to draw over all transferred lines and to write ". . . have a sunshine day!!" on cloud. Use blue highlighter to draw over lines on cloud and pink highlighter to draw over lines on sun. Glue cloud to sun. Punch hole in tag.
3. Line basket with towel; place gift in basket. Gather towel around gift; secure with rubber band. Tie 1"w ribbon into a bow around gathers to cover rubber band. Use 1/16"w ribbon to tie tag to bow. Knot remaining ribbons around knot of bow.

CUPCAKE SURPRISE

*S*urprise a terrific family with a bag of our Spicy Granola Cupcake Mix! It's a cinch to toss together, and delivery is easy when you pack it in a handmade fabric bag. A silk flower and an appliquéd recipe card complete the cheerful gift.

SPICY GRANOLA CUPCAKE MIX

1 package (18¼ ounces) yellow cake mix
2 cups granola cereal with nuts and dried fruit
1 teaspoon ground cinnamon
⅛ teaspoon ground cloves

In a large bowl, combine cake mix, cereal, cinnamon, and cloves. Divide mixture into 2 resealable plastic bags (about 2½ cups in each bag). Give with baking instructions.

Yield: about 5 cups mix

To bake: Preheat oven to 350 degrees. Combine bag of cupcake mix, ⅔ cup water, 2 eggs, and 2 tablespoons oil in a medium bowl; beat until well blended. Fill paper-lined muffin cups about three-fourths full. Bake 18 to 20 minutes or until a toothpick inserted in center of cupcake comes out clean and tops are golden brown. Serve warm.

Yield: about 1 dozen cupcakes

FLORAL BAG AND TAG

You will need a 7½" x 32" piece of flower-motif fabric, ¾"w paper-backed fusible web tape, 1¾" x 32" torn fabric strip, silk flower, and a hot glue gun.
For gift tag, you will *also* need flower-motif fabric, craft glue, 4" x 6" index

card, ½" x 6" fabric strip, black permanent fine-point marker, hole punch, and jute twine.

1. For bag, matching right sides and short edges, fold fabric in half. Using a ¼" seam allowance, sew sides of bag together.
2. Follow manufacturer's instructions to fuse web tape to wrong side along top edge of bag. Do not remove paper backing. Press edge 3" to wrong side; unfold and remove paper backing. Refold

edge and fuse in place. Turn bag right side out.
3. Place gift in bag. Tie fabric strip into a bow around top of bag; notch ends. Hot glue flower to knot of bow.
4. For gift tag, cut desired motifs from fabric. Use craft glue to glue fabric strip and motifs to card. Use marker to add details along edges of tag and to write baking instructions on tag. Punch hole in tag. Use twine to attach tag to bow.

Share the citrusy sweetness of Orange Slice Cookies with someone who's a "ray of sunshine" in your life! These delicious munchies make a great get-well or secret pal gift. A wooden crate embellished with a bright craft foam sun and an uplifting message add to the fun of this perky offering.

ORANGE SLICE COOKIES

COOKIES

- 1 cup butter or margarine, softened
- 1 cup granulated sugar
- $^1/_2$ cup confectioners sugar
- 1 egg
- 1 teaspoon orange extract
- $^1/_4$ teaspoon orange paste food coloring
- 2$^1/_2$ cups all-purpose flour
- $^1/_2$ teaspoon baking powder
- $^1/_4$ teaspoon salt

ICING

- $^3/_4$ cup confectioners sugar
- 1 tablespoon butter or margarine
- 1 tablespoon vegetable shortening
- $^1/_4$ teaspoon vanilla extract
- $^1/_8$ teaspoon orange extract
- 1 to 2 teaspoons milk

Preheat oven to 375 degrees. For cookies, cream butter and sugars in a large bowl until fluffy. Add egg, orange extract, and food coloring; beat until smooth. In a medium bowl, combine flour, baking powder, and salt. Add dry ingredients to creamed mixture; stir until a soft dough forms. On a lightly floured surface, use a floured rolling pin to roll out dough to $^1/_4$-inch thickness. Use a 3-inch-diameter round cookie cutter to cut out cookies. Cut each cookie in half. Place cookies 2 inches apart on a greased baking sheet. Using a table knife, make indentations in cookies to resemble orange segments. Bake 7 to 9 minutes or until bottoms are lightly browned. Transfer cookies to a wire rack to cool.

For icing, combine confectioners sugar, butter, shortening, extracts, and milk in a small bowl; beat until smooth. Transfer icing to a pastry bag fitted with a small round tip. Pipe outline onto each cookie. Let icing harden. Store in an airtight container.

Yield: about 5 dozen cookies

SLICE OF SUNSHINE BASKET

You will need tracing paper, yellow and orange craft foam, white poster board, drawing compass, low temperature glue gun, transfer paper, black permanent fine-point marker, white acrylic paint, small paintbrush, 22" of $^5/_8$"w yellow ribbon, quart-size wooden produce basket, natural wood excelsior, cellophane, and 8$^1/_2$" of $^3/_8$"w yellow ribbon.

1. Trace patterns, this page, onto tracing paper. Use patterns to cut sun rays from orange foam and tag from poster board. For sun, use compass to draw a 2" dia. circle on yellow foam; cut out. Center and glue sun on sun rays.
2. Use transfer paper to transfer face to sun and words to tag. Use marker to draw over transferred lines and to color pupils of eyes. Paint white areas of each eye; allow to dry.
3. Overlapping ends at back, glue $^5/_8$"w ribbon around rim of basket.
4. Glue sun and tag to front of basket.
5. Line bottom of basket with excelsior. Place cookies on cellophane. Gather cellophane over cookies. Knot $^3/_8$"w ribbon around gathers. Place gift in basket.

SUMMERTIME SIPPER

*M*ade with real fruit, our Watermelon Coolers will help beat the summertime heat — one sip at a time! Deliver a canister of the concentrate along with lemon-lime soda in a cute sponge-painted gift bag. Be sure to include serving instructions for the ready-to-mix spritzer.

WATERMELON COOLERS

  6 cups seeded watermelon pieces (about a 5-pound watermelon)
  1 cup boiling water
  ¹/₄ cup watermelon gelatin
  1 bottle (1 liter) chilled lemon-lime soda to serve

Process watermelon pieces in a food processor until puréed (about 4 cups). Press through a sieve or food mill; discard pulp. In a small bowl, combine boiling water and gelatin; stir until gelatin dissolves. In a 1¹/₂-quart container, combine gelatin mixture and watermelon purée. Cover and refrigerate. Give with lemon-lime soda and serving instructions.

Yield: about 5 cups cooler concentrate

To serve: In a 3-quart container, combine watermelon cooler concentrate and soda. Serve chilled.

Yield: about 9 cups cooler

WATERMELON BAG

You will need a large brown paper bag; white, pink, red, green, dark green, and black acrylic paint; craft sponge; paintbrush; 1¹/₂" yds. of 1¹/₂"w craft ribbon; craft wire; wire cutters; hot glue gun; and green excelsior.

Follow Painting Techniques, page 122, for painting tips.

1. Fold top of bag 1³/₄" to outside twice.
2. Applying each color while paint is still wet, follow *Sponge Painting*, page 122, using white, green, and dark green paint to paint fold of bag. Using white, pink, and red paint, repeat to paint front of bag.
3. Use black paint and paintbrush to paint seeds on bag.
4. Follow *Making a Bow*, page 121, to make a bow with seven 6" loops, two 4¹/₂" streamers, and a 2" center loop. Glue bow to bag.
5. Line bag with excelsior. Place gifts in bag.

CREAMY STRAWBERRY SOUP

*S*ay "Thanks!" in a big way with a batch of Creamy Strawberry Soup delivered in a cute berry pitcher. Served chilled, this refreshing soup combines fresh berries and flavored liqueur for a spirited way to show your appreciation.

CREAMY STRAWBERRY SOUP

1 quart fresh strawberries, capped and sliced
4 ounces cream cheese, softened
$1/2$ cup sugar
1 container (8 ounces) lemon yogurt
3 cups half and half
$1/2$ cup strawberry-flavored liqueur

Process strawberries, cream cheese, and sugar in a food processor until smooth. Add yogurt and pulse process until blended. Transfer mixture to a large bowl; whisk in half and half and liqueur. Cover and chill 2 hours to let flavors blend before serving. Serve chilled.

Yield: about 8 cups soup

THANKS "BERRY" MUCH GIFT TAG

You will need tracing paper, green paper, yellow colored pencil, black permanent fine-point marker, hole punch, hot glue gun, green curling ribbon, and small silk flowers.

1. Trace pattern, page 110, onto tracing paper. Use pattern to cut leaf from green paper.

2. Use pencil to shade edges and draw veins on leaf. Use marker to write message on tag. Punch hole in tag.

3. Use curling ribbon to attach tag to gift; curl ribbon ends. Glue flowers to tag.

43

Our "catch of the day" appetizer basket is a great way to greet the hostess! Complete with nutty homemade crackers, veggie pickles, and a spicy cheese ball, the delicious snack combination will "reel in" lots of hungry friends. Finish with splashy curled ribbon and a fun fish tag.

SPICY CORNMEAL CRACKERS

CRACKERS
- 2 cups all-purpose flour
- 1 cup yellow cornmeal
- 1 cup chopped pecans, toasted and finely ground
- 1 teaspoon salt
- 1 teaspoon garlic salt
- 1/2 teaspoon ground cumin
- 1/2 teaspoon ground red pepper
- 1 cup butter-flavored vegetable shortening
- 6 to 7 tablespoons water

TOPPING
- 1 tablespoon yellow cornmeal
- 1/4 teaspoon ground cumin
- 1/4 teaspoon salt

Preheat oven to 350 degrees. For crackers, combine flour, cornmeal, pecans, salt, garlic salt, cumin, and red pepper in a large bowl. Using a pastry blender or 2 knives, cut in shortening until mixture resembles coarse meal. Sprinkle with water, 1 tablespoon at a time, stirring until mixture clings together and a soft dough forms. Divide dough into thirds. Working with one third of dough at a time, place dough on a sheet of aluminum foil. Cover with plastic wrap and roll out dough to a 12-inch square.

Cut dough into 2-inch squares; do not separate.

For topping, combine cornmeal, cumin, and salt in a small bowl. Sprinkle about 1 teaspoon topping over each sheet of crackers. Prick each cracker 3 times with a fork. Transfer crackers on foil to a baking sheet. Bake 23 to 25 minutes or until lightly browned. Transfer crackers to a wire rack to cool. Store in a cookie tin.

Yield: about 8 dozen crackers

BEEFY CHEESE BALL

For a saltier taste, do not rinse dried beef.

- 1 package (8 ounces) cream cheese, softened
- 1/4 cup finely chopped green onions
- 1 jar (2¼ ounces) dried beef, rinsed and coarsely chopped
- 1 tablespoon Worcestershire sauce
- 1 clove garlic, minced
- 1/2 teaspoon lemon pepper
- 2/3 cup finely chopped pecans

In a medium bowl, beat cream cheese until smooth. Add onions, beef, Worcestershire sauce, garlic, and lemon pepper; beat until blended. Cover and chill 3 hours.

With greased hands, shape mixture into a ball. Press pecans onto cheese ball. Wrap in plastic wrap and chill overnight to let flavors blend.

Yield: 1 cheese ball, about 1⅓ cups

VEGGIE PICKLES

- 6 cups cauliflower flowerets
- 1 package (16 ounces) peeled baby carrots (about 3½ cups)
- 3 cups 1-inch-long celery pieces
- 2 cups fresh pearl onions, peeled
- 1 cup small red cherry peppers
- 1/3 cup canning and pickling salt

- 4 cups sugar
- 2 cups apple cider vinegar
- 1/2 cup water
- 1 tablespoon pickling spice
- 6 cloves garlic

In a 4-quart nonmetal bowl, combine cauliflower, carrots, celery, onions, and peppers. Sprinkle with canning salt. Add water to cover vegetables. Cover and let stand 1 hour. Drain well. Rinse with cold water and drain again.

In a large Dutch oven, combine sugar, vinegar, water, and pickling spice. Add vegetables to liquid. Stirring frequently, cook over high heat until mixture comes to a boil. Spoon vegetables into 6 heat-resistant 1-pint jars. Add a garlic clove to each jar. Carefully pour hot liquid over vegetables. Cover and cool to room temperature. Store in refrigerator.

Yield: about 12 cups pickles

FABULOUS CATCH BASKET

You will need fabric to line basket and a basket (we used a 9" square basket with ceramic fish handles).

For gift tag, you will *also* need tracing paper, transfer paper, poster board, black permanent fine-point marker, colored pencils, 15" of lightweight craft wire, and a hot glue gun.

1. Arrange fabric in basket.
2. For gift tag, trace fish pattern, page 110, onto tracing paper. Use transfer paper to transfer fish design to poster board. Use marker to draw over all transferred lines. Use pencils to color design. Leaving a 1/8" border, cut out fish tag.
3. Twist wire around pencil to curl; remove from pencil. Glue tag to one end of wire. Use wire to attach tag to gift.

CAUGHT IN A PICKLE

*S*ay "Thanks!" to a friend for helping you out of a "pickle" with crisp Pickled Green Beans. The recipe makes several pints, so you can keep the extras on hand for last-minute gifts. Add a hand-colored label, then follow our simple instructions to create a ribbon-handled "tote."

PICKLED GREEN BEANS

15 cups water, divided
 3 pounds fresh green beans, washed and ends removed
 5 cloves garlic
 5 sprigs fresh dill weed *or* 5 teaspoons dried dill weed
 5 small dried hot red peppers *or* $2^{1}/_2$ teaspoons crushed red pepper flakes
$1^{1}/_4$ cups white vinegar (5% acidity)
 $^{1}/_4$ cup plus 2 teaspoons canning and pickling salt

In a large Dutch oven, bring 12 cups water to a boil over high heat. Add green beans and bring to a boil again; cook 7 minutes. Drain and place beans in ice water to stop cooking process. Drain and pack beans vertically in five 1-pint heat-resistant jars with lids. Place 1 garlic clove, 1 sprig dill weed, and 1 small red pepper in each jar. In a large non-aluminum saucepan, bring vinegar, remaining 3 cups water, and canning salt to a boil over high heat. Pour hot vinegar mixture into jars. Cover and cool jars to room temperature. Refrigerate at least 1 week before serving to let flavors blend. Store in refrigerator.

Yield: 5 pints green beans

"PICKLED" PRESENT

You will need colored pencils, photocopy of label design (page 110), craft glue, pint-size canning jar with lid, felt, poster board, and 21" of $1^{1}/_2$"w ribbon.

1. Use pencils to color label; cut out. Glue label to jar.
2. For jar lid insert, remove lid from jar. Draw around flat part of lid on felt and poster board; cut out inside drawn lines. Glue felt circle to poster board circle.
3. Before presenting gift, remove band from jar. Place insert felt side up on flat part of jar lid. Position center of ribbon across insert. Replace band on jar. Knot ribbon ends together to form handle.

GARDEN-HERB VINEGAR

EXTRA easy!

Capture the essence of fresh-picked herbs with a bottle of tasty Tarragon Vinegar. The zippy condiment is a delicious topping for homegrown salads and steamed veggies. Dress the container in a miniature apron and tiny sprigs of flowers for delivering the well-seasoned gift to your neighborhood gardener.

TARRAGON VINEGAR

  8 sprigs of fresh tarragon, washed, patted dry, and lightly crushed
  2 cloves garlic, crushed
  $^1/_4$ teaspoon crushed red pepper flakes
  4 cups white wine vinegar

Place tarragon, garlic, and red pepper flakes in a 1-quart glass container. In a medium non-aluminum saucepan, bring vinegar to a boil over high heat. Pour vinegar over mixture. Cover and let stand at room temperature 1 week.

Strain mixture into gift bottles. Store in refrigerator up to 1 month.

Yield: about 4 cups vinegar

DECORATED BOTTLE APRON

You will need artificial flower sprigs, hot glue gun, and an apron with "flowerpot" pockets to fit on bottle.

For tag, you will *also* need a black permanent fine-point marker, 1¹/₂" x 2" piece of handmade paper, ¹/₈" dia. hole punch, and a 6" twig.

1. Arrange and glue flowers in pockets.
2. For tag, use marker to draw "stitches" along edges of paper piece and to write message on tag. Punch a hole at center of each short edge.

3. Thread twig through holes in tag; glue twig in one pocket.

TICKLED PINK

*W*hen young ladies gather
for sleep-over fun, they'll be
tickled pink with these candy-
filled lipstick party favors! The
oversize "cosmetics" are created
with gift-wrapped cardboard
tubes and bright plastic eggs.

LIPSTICK PARTY FAVORS

For each party favor, you will need gold
wrapping paper, spray adhesive, $1^5/8$" dia.
plastic egg, $4^1/2$" of $1^5/8$" dia. cardboard
tube, poster board, hot glue gun, 6" of
$5/8$"w gold trim, assorted candies to fill
tube, drawing compass, and 18" of $3/8$"w
gold mesh wired ribbon.

*Use hot glue for all gluing unless
otherwise indicated.*

1. Cut a 5" x 6" piece from wrapping
paper. Apply spray adhesive to wrong side
of paper. Overlapping long edges at back,
smooth paper around tube. Fold excess
paper to inside of tube, clipping ends
as necessary.
2. For top, insert egg inside tube so that
pointed end of egg extends beyond
opposite end of tube; glue to secure. Fill
tube with candy.
3. Overlapping ends at back, glue trim
around bottom edge of tube. Use compass
to draw a 2" dia. circle on poster board
and a $2^1/2$" dia. circle on wrapping paper;
cut out. Apply spray adhesive to wrong
side of paper circle. Center poster board
circle on wrong side of paper circle;
smooth edges of paper circle over poster
board circle. Glue covered circle to
bottom of tube.
4. Tie ribbon into a bow around tube.

BLACKBERRY-MINT VINEGAR

*B*ring distinctive flavor to the table with Blackberry-Mint Vinegar. The tart condiment is great for salads. For an elegant presentation, pour the vinegar into a stylish etched bottle wrapped with ribbon and faux berries.

BLACKBERRY-MINT VINEGAR

　5　cups white vinegar
　2　cups fresh or frozen whole
　　　　blackberries
$1/3$　cup sugar
$1/8$　teaspoon salt
　8　fresh mint leaves

In a large non-aluminum saucepan, combine vinegar, blackberries, sugar, and salt. Bring to a boil over medium-high heat; boil 3 minutes. Add mint leaves. Transfer mixture to a heatproof nonmetal container. Cover and let stand at room temperature 3 days to let flavors blend.

Strain vinegar into gift bottles. Store in refrigerator up to 1 month.

Yield: about $5^1/4$ cups vinegar

BERRY-ETCHED BOTTLE

You will need a permanent fine-point marker, clear Con-Tact® paper, craft knife, cutting mat, clean dry bottle with cork, newspaper, plastic gloves, etching cream, paintbrush, gold rub-on metallic finish, soft cloth, 18" of $1^3/8$"w mesh wired ribbon, and a 10" wired artificial berry sprig.

1. For stencil, use permanent marker to trace berry design, page 111, onto Con-Tact® paper. Leaving a $1/2$" border around design, use craft knife to cut out

stencil. Remove paper backing and smooth stencil on bottle.
2. Follow manufacturer's instructions to apply etching cream to bottle.
3. Remove etching cream and stencil.

4. Follow manufacturer's instructions to apply gold finish to design; allow to dry. Gently buff design with cloth (gold will adhere to etched surface).
5. Tie ribbon into a bow around neck of bottle. Insert berry sprig under bow.

49

Spice up a friend's cookout with these super sauces! Included are toppings for all kinds of tastes — zesty Mustard-Cheese Spread, rich Blue Cheese Topping, and creamy Hamburger Sauce. Pack the condiments, along with plates and napkins, in a hand-painted "watermelon" crate for a summery surprise.

MUSTARD-CHEESE SPREAD

  2 jars (8 ounces each) pasteurized process cheese sauce
1/4 cup prepared mustard

In a small bowl, combine cheese sauce and mustard; stir until smooth. Store in an airtight container in refrigerator.

Yield: about 2 cups sauce

BLUE CHEESE TOPPING

3/4 cup sour cream
3/4 cup blue cheese salad dressing
3/4 cup crumbled blue cheese
  6 tablespoons cooked and finely chopped bacon (about 8 slices)

In a small bowl, combine sour cream, salad dressing, and blue cheese; stir until well blended. Stir in bacon. Store in an airtight container.

Yield: about 2 cups topping

HAMBURGER SAUCE

  2 cups mayonnaise
2/3 cup Thousand Island salad dressing
  2 tablespoons sweet pickle relish
1/2 teaspoon dried minced onion
1/4 teaspoon ground black pepper

In a small bowl, combine mayonnaise, salad dressing, relish, onion, and black pepper; whisk until well blended. Store in an airtight container in refrigerator.

Yield: about 2½ cups sauce

WATERMELON CRATE AND LABELS

You will need a wooden crate with rounded ends (we used a 9" x 12" crate); white, red, light green, green, and black acrylic paint; paintbrushes; and fabric to line basket.

For labels, you will *also* need tracing paper, transfer paper, poster board, black permanent fine-point marker, colored pencils, hot glue gun, three plastic spoons, three 1" x 12" torn fabric strips, green floral wire, wire cutters, and three pint-size plastic containers.

Follow Painting Techniques, page 122, for painting tips. Allow paint to dry after each application.

1. Draw a line 1/4" from round edge on outside of each end of crate. Leaving outside of ends of crate below line unpainted, paint crate green.
2. For watermelon design on each end, paint a 1/4"w light green stripe below green area; paint remaining area red. Paint black seeds with white highlights.
3. Arrange fabric in crate.
4. For labels, trace watermelon slice pattern, this page, onto tracing paper. Use transfer paper to transfer three watermelon slices to poster board. Use marker to draw over transferred lines and to write one recipe name on each watermelon slice. Use pencils to color labels; cut out.
5. Glue one label to each spoon handle. Tie one fabric strip into a bow around each spoon handle. Use wire to attach spoon to container.

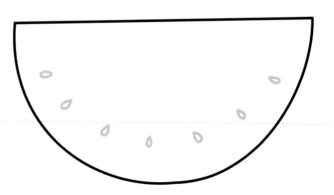

VICTORIAN CANDY BOXES

*Y*ou won't believe how easy it is to whip up these rich chocolate candies! Pudding mix makes them quick, and the recipe provides enough for several friends. Plain white boxes become romantic packages when decorated with Victorian stickers, ribbon, and silk flowers.

NUTTY CHOCOLATE CHUNKS

1 cup sugar
1 package (3.4 ounces) chocolate pudding mix (do not use instant)
1 can (5 ounces) evaporated milk
2 tablespoons butter or margarine
1 teaspoon almond extract
2/3 cup sliced almonds, toasted and coarsely chopped

Line an 8-inch square baking pan with aluminum foil, extending foil over 2 sides of pan; grease foil. In a medium saucepan, combine sugar, pudding mix, and milk. Stirring constantly over medium heat, bring mixture to a full boil; boil 5 minutes. Remove from heat. Stir in butter and almond extract. Pour mixture into a medium bowl. Beat with an electric mixer at high speed about 6 minutes or until mixture thickens and begins to lose its gloss. Stir in almonds. Pour into prepared pan. Chill 2 hours or until firm.

Use ends of foil to lift candy from pan. Cut into 1-inch squares. Store in an airtight container in refrigerator.

Yield: about 4 dozen candies

VICTORIAN GIFT BOXES

You will need a hot glue gun, purchased boxes with handles (we used 3"w x 4"h x 3"d white boxes), assorted trims (we used ribbon and braid), Victorian-motif stickers, assorted ribbons, floral wire, wire cutters, artificial greenery, silk flowers, purchased 2" x 3" gift tags, black medium-point permanent marker, and double-sided tape.

1. For each box, glue desired trims around box. Apply stickers to box.
2. Place gift in box.
3. Use ribbon and follow *Making a Bow*, page 121, to make a bow with desired number and size of loops and streamers. Wire bow to handle. Glue flowers or greenery to knot of bow.
4. Write message on tag; tape tag to box.

CLEARLY ELEGANT

*T*opped off with a glittery bow, our elegant gift bag makes it clear to see that it's filled with something really sweet! These moist Chocolate-Coconut Bars give you a head start on preparation with a packaged cake mix. What a delightful way to show you care!

CHOCOLATE-COCONUT BARS

  1 package (18¼ ounces) chocolate cake mix with pudding in the mix
  ⅓ cup unsalted butter or margarine, softened
  1 egg
  1½ cups flaked coconut
  1 cup slivered almonds, toasted and coarsely chopped
  ¾ cup semisweet chocolate mini chips
  ½ cup firmly packed brown sugar
  ½ cup granulated sugar
  1 egg
  ¼ cup cream of coconut
  2 tablespoons all-purpose flour
  1 teaspoon vanilla extract

Preheat oven to 325 degrees. Line a 9 x 13-inch baking pan with aluminum foil, extending foil over ends of pan; grease foil. In a medium bowl, combine cake mix, butter, and 1 egg; beat until well blended (mixture will be crumbly). Firmly press mixture into bottom of prepared pan. Sprinkle coconut, almonds, and chocolate chips over crust. In a medium bowl, combine sugars and 1 egg; beat until smooth. Add cream of coconut, flour, and vanilla; beat just until blended. Spread mixture into pan. Bake 28 to

32 minutes or until set and lightly browned. Cool in pan on a wire rack.

Use ends of foil to lift from pan. Cut into 2-inch squares. Store in an airtight container in a cool place.

Yield: about 2 dozen bars

BERIBBONED GIFT BAG

You will need a cellophane gift bag (we used a 2¾" x 10" clear cellophane bag with gold and white designs) and 28" of 2⅜"w sheer wired ribbon.

Place gift in bag. Tie ribbon into a bow around top of bag.

"ORANGE" YOU GLAD!

*T*his light, fluffy treat is just right for sharing between friends. A creamy blend of fruity flavors, Apricot-Orange Chiffon Pie is easy to stir up with simple ingredients. Place the pie in a fabric-lined basket, wrap with cellophane, and top it off with a clever craft foam tag.

APRICOT-ORANGE CHIFFON PIE

CRUST

1¼ cups all-purpose flour
½ teaspoon salt
½ teaspoon grated orange zest
⅓ cup vegetable shortening
3 to 4 tablespoons cold orange juice

FILLING

1 can (15¼ ounces) apricot halves in heavy syrup
1 package (3 ounces) apricot gelatin
½ teaspoon orange extract
¼ teaspoon salt
1 cup half and half
1 package (3.4 ounces) vanilla instant pudding mix
1 container (8 ounces) frozen non-dairy whipped topping, thawed

Preheat oven to 400 degrees. For crust, combine flour, salt, and orange zest in a medium bowl. Using a pastry blender or 2 knives, cut in shortening until mixture resembles coarse meal. Sprinkle with orange juice; mix until a soft dough forms. On a lightly floured surface, use a floured rolling pin to roll out dough. Transfer to a 9-inch pie plate and use a sharp knife to trim edge of dough. Flute edge of dough. Prick bottom of crust with a fork. Bake 15 to 18 minutes or until golden brown. Cool completely on a wire rack.

For filling, drain apricots, reserving syrup. Place reserved apricot syrup (about ¾ cup) in a small saucepan. Stirring constantly, add gelatin and cook over medium-low heat about 8 minutes or until gelatin dissolves. Transfer to a large bowl; cool at room temperature 30 minutes.

Process drained apricots, orange extract, and salt in a food processor until apricots are puréed. Add to gelatin mixture. In a small bowl, combine half and half and pudding mix; beat according to package directions. Add to fruit mixture; beat until smooth. Fold in whipped topping. Spoon filling into crust. Cover and chill about 2 hours or until firm. Serve chilled.

Yield: about 8 servings

"GLAD WE'RE FRIENDS" TAG

You will need a drawing compass; orange, red, green, and black craft foam; tracing paper; white poster board; hole punch; low temperature glue gun; black permanent fine-point marker; red colored pencil; toothpick; white acrylic paint; craft wire; wire cutters; 1 yd. of 1½"w white satin wired ribbon; and cellophane.

Allow paint and craft glue to dry after each application.

1. For orange, use compass to draw a 2½" dia. circle on orange craft foam; cut out.
2. Trace patterns, this page, onto tracing paper; cut out. Use patterns to cut two leaves from green craft foam, one heart from red craft foam, and one tag from poster board. Punch two holes from black craft foam for eyes.
3. For "face" on orange, glue eyes to orange. Use marker to draw eyelashes and mouth. Glue heart to center of mouth. Use pencil to add cheeks and to shade edge of orange. Use toothpick to make "dimples" in orange. Use toothpick and paint to add a white highlight to each eye.
4. Glue leaves to top of orange.
5. Glue tag to orange craft foam. Use marker to write message on tag. Leaving a ⅛" orange border, cut out tag. Glue orange "face" to tag.
6. Use ribbon and follow *Making a Bow*, page 121, to make a bow with six 8" loops and two 2" streamers.
7. Gather cellophane around pie; twist wire ends at back of bow around gathers to secure.
8. Glue tag to bow.

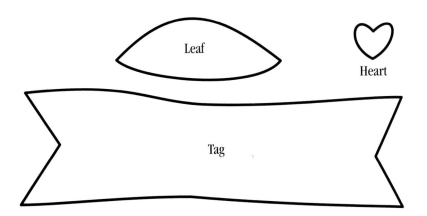

Leaf

Heart

Tag

FUDGE FOR FATHER

*M*ake Dad's Day *delightful with a gift of Spicy Date-Nut Fudge — it's packed with yummy bits of dates and coconut. Deliver a batch in a handsome gift box that's cleverly covered with a shirt front for a "well-suited" presentation!*

SPICY DATE-NUT FUDGE

 3 cups sugar
 3/4 cup butter or margarine
 1 can (5 ounces) evaporated milk
 1 jar (7 ounces) marshmallow creme
 1 package (6 ounces) semisweet chocolate chips
 1 teaspoon vanilla extract
 1 teaspoon ground cinnamon
 1/2 teaspoon ground allspice
 1 package (8 ounces) chopped dates
 1 cup chopped pecans, toasted
 1 cup flaked coconut

Line a 9-inch square baking pan with aluminum foil, extending foil over 2 sides of pan; grease foil. Butter sides of a heavy large saucepan. Combine sugar, butter, and evaporated milk in saucepan. Stirring constantly, bring mixture to a boil over medium heat; boil 5 minutes. Remove from heat. Add marshmallow creme, chocolate chips, vanilla, cinnamon, and allspice; stir until chips melt. Stir in dates, pecans, and coconut. Pour mixture into prepared pan. Chill about 2 hours or until firm.

Use ends of foil to lift fudge from pan. Cut into 1-inch squares. Store in an airtight container in refrigerator.

Yield: about 5 dozen pieces fudge

GENTLEMAN'S GIFT BOX

You will need an 11½" square of fusible interfacing, man's button-front shirt with pocket, 9" square x 1½"h papier-mâché box, craft glue, paper-backed fusible web, and two neckties.

For gift tag, you will *also* need white card stock, decorative-edge craft scissors, and a black permanent fine-point marker.

Allow glue to dry after each application.

1. Center interfacing over placket and pocket on shirt front. Using interfacing as a pattern, cut out shirt piece. Follow manufacturer's instructions to fuse interfacing to wrong side of shirt piece.

2. Center lid on wrong side of fused shirt. Folding shirt edges to inside of lid and pleating corners as necessary, glue edges to inside of lid.

3. Use pattern, page 110, and follow *Making Appliqués*, page 122, to make one heart appliqué from one necktie fabric and one 2½" x 3¾" appliqué from remaining necktie fabric. Fuse heart appliqué to shirt pocket.

4. For tag, fuse 2½" x 3¾" appliqué to card stock; cut out along edges of fabric. Use craft scissors to cut a 2" x 3" piece from card stock; glue to fabric side of tag. Use marker to write message on tag.

DUCKY DAD'S DAY

*T*his Father's Day gift will let someone know he's one "ducky" dad! Easy to prepare, Creamy Chocolate Pecan Pie is delicious when served chilled. Tuck it in a basket that's dressed up with a handsome bow and a miniature duck decoy for a sporty touch.

CREAMY CHOCOLATE PECAN PIE

- 1 package (8 ounces) cream cheese, softened
- $3/4$ cup sugar
- 3 eggs
- $3/4$ cup light corn syrup
- $1/3$ cup cocoa
- 2 tablespoons all-purpose flour
- 1 teaspoon vanilla extract
- $1/2$ teaspoon salt
- $1^1/2$ cups chopped pecans
- 1 unbaked deep-dish 9-inch pie crust

Preheat oven to 350 degrees. In a medium bowl, beat cream cheese and sugar until fluffy. Add eggs, corn syrup, cocoa, flour, vanilla, and salt; beat until well blended. Stir in pecans. Pour into pie crust. Bake 55 to 60 minutes or until a knife inserted near center comes out clean. If edge of crust browns too quickly, cover with a strip of aluminum foil. Cool on a wire rack. Cover and chill 2 hours. Serve chilled.

Yield: about 8 servings

LUCKY DUCK BASKET

You will need 2 yds. of $2^5/8$"w ribbon, 10" dia. basket with handle, green floral wire, wire cutters, hot glue gun, $2^3/4$"h wooden duck, and an 18" square of fabric with pinked edge for liner.

1. Cut a 10" length from ribbon. Use remaining ribbon and follow *Making a Bow,* page 121, to make a bow with six 8" loops, one 5" streamer, and one 3" streamer. Use 10" length of ribbon to attach bow to basket handle; notch ends.

2. Glue duck to center of bow.

3. Place liner in basket.

SALT OF THE EARTH

EXTRA easy!

F̲riends are the spice of life, so why not tell them so? This special blend of herbs and seasonings takes the place of ordinary table salt. Toted in a cute hanging basket, a shaker of the salt makes a "tasteful" token.

SPECIAL SEASONING SALT

Use seasoning salt in place of table salt.

- 1 cup salt
- 2 teaspoons paprika
- 1 teaspoon dry mustard
- 1 teaspoon garlic powder
- 1 teaspoon onion powder
- $1/2$ teaspoon ground oregano leaves
- $1/2$ teaspoon ground thyme leaves
- $1/2$ teaspoon curry powder
- $1/2$ teaspoon dried dill weed
- $1/2$ teaspoon celery seed

In a small bowl, combine salt, paprika, dry mustard, garlic powder, onion powder, oregano, thyme, curry powder, dill weed, and celery seed. Store in an airtight container.

Yield: about $1^1/4$ cups seasoning salt

"SALT OF THE EARTH" BASKET

You will need $1^1/2$" x 12" torn fabric strip, hot glue gun, a small basket (we used a $4^1/2$" dia. x 5"h hanging basket), silk flower, natural wood excelsior, and a salt shaker (we used a $3^7/8$"h x $2^3/4$" dia. shaker).
For tag, you will *also* need tracing paper, handmade paper, craft glue, card stock, brown permanent fine-point marker, and a craft stick.

1. Tie fabric strip into a bow; glue to front of basket. Hot glue flower to knot of bow. Line basket with excelsior.
2. For tag, trace pattern, page 111, onto tracing paper; cut out. Draw around heart on handmade paper. Carefully tear heart along drawn line. Use craft glue to glue heart to card stock. Leaving a narrow border, cut out tag.
3. Use marker to write message on tag. Glue tag to one end of craft stick; place in basket.
4. Fill shaker with seasoning salt and place in basket.

58

FOURTH OF JULY FUDGE BARS

*H*ere's a sizzling idea
for patriotic giving! A batch
of Crunchy Fudge Bars is a
delicious offering to share
with friends and neighbors at
the holiday picnic. Carry the
tempting treats in a rustic
all-American crate to wish
everyone a fabulous Fourth!

CRUNCHY FUDGE BARS

1 package (22½ ounces) fudge
   brownie mix and ingredients to
   prepare brownies
1 cup coarsely chopped salted
   peanuts
2 packages (3 ounces each) cream
   cheese, softened
¼ cup crunchy peanut butter
1 egg
1 package (16 ounces) chocolate-
   flavored confectioners sugar
¾ cup almond brickle chips

Preheat oven to 350 degrees. Line a
10½ x 15½-inch jellyroll pan with
aluminum foil, extending foil over ends of
pan; grease foil. Prepare brownie batter
according to package directions. Stir in
peanuts. Spread batter into prepared pan.
In a medium bowl, beat cream cheese
and peanut butter until fluffy. Add egg;
beat until smooth. Gradually add
confectioners sugar and beat until
smooth. Spread over batter. Sprinkle with
brickle chips. Bake 30 to 34 minutes or
until center is almost set. Cool in pan.

Use ends of foil to lift brownies from
pan. Cut into 2-inch squares. Store in an
airtight container.

Yield: about 3 dozen brownies

RUSTIC ALL-AMERICAN CRATE

You will need white, red, and blue acrylic
paint; paintbrushes; one 5½"w and two
4"w wooden hearts; foam brush; wood
stain; soft cloth; wooden crate with handle
(we used an 8" x 13½" x 3½"d crate);
hot glue gun; fabric for basket liner; 28"
of brown paper twist (4½"w untwisted);
and a 1⅛" dia. button.
For gift tag, you will *also* need a black
permanent fine-point marker, 2" square
of cream-colored card stock, 2½" square
of tan card stock, hole punch, and
jute twine.

*Follow Painting Techniques, page 122,
for painting tips. Allow paint to dry
after each application.*

1. Use paint to freehand flag design on
each heart.
2. Use foam brush to apply wood stain to
hearts and crate. Wipe with cloth to
remove excess stain; allow to dry.
3. Glue hearts to side of crate.
4. Follow *Making a Basket Liner,*
page 121, to make liner with an
unfinished edge; place in crate.
5. Tie paper twist into a bow around
handle. Glue button to knot of bow.
6. For gift tag, use marker to write
message on cream-colored card stock;
draw "stitches" along inside edges. Center
and glue tag to tan card stock.
7. Punch hole in tag. Use twine to hang
tag on button.

YANKEE-DOODLE MACAROONS

A *basket cushioned with star-spangled fabric provides a patriotic platter for these bite-size cookies. Made in minutes using packaged baking mix, Easy Coconut Macaroons are studded with colorful candied cherries for a treat that neighbors will salute!*

EASY COCONUT MACAROONS

2 cups all-purpose baking mix
1 can (14 ounces) sweetened
    condensed milk
1 egg
1 teaspoon vanilla extract
1 can (3½ ounces) flaked coconut
    Vegetable cooking spray
2 tablespoons sugar
5 ounces red candied cherries,
    halved

Preheat oven to 350 degrees. In a large bowl, combine baking mix, sweetened condensed milk, egg, and vanilla; beat until well blended. Stir in coconut. Drop teaspoonfuls of dough onto a cookie sheet sprayed with cooking spray. Sprinkle tops of cookies with sugar. Bake 6 to 8 minutes or until bottoms are golden brown. Press a cherry half into center of each warm cookie. Transfer cookies to a wire rack to cool. Store in an airtight container.

Yield: about 6 dozen cookies

FESTIVE FOURTH OF JULY BASKET

You will need a round basket (we used a 7½" dia. x 4½"h basket); blue fabric to cover basket; string; fabric marking pencil; thumbtack; embroidery floss; polyester fiberfill; hot glue gun; rubber band; ¼"w white, ⅜"w blue, and ⅝"w red satin ribbons; 1½" dia. liberty bell; gold star garland; and red fabric to line basket.

1. Measure basket from rim to rim (Fig. 1); add 9". Cut a square of blue fabric the determined measurement.

Fig. 1

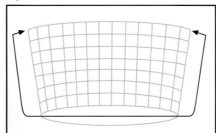

2. Matching right sides, fold square in half from top to bottom and again from left to right. Tie one end of string to fabric marking pencil. Measure ½ the measurement determined in Step 1 from pencil; insert thumbtack through string at this point. Insert thumbtack through fabric and mark cutting line (Fig. 2). Cutting through all layers, cut out circle.

Fig. 2

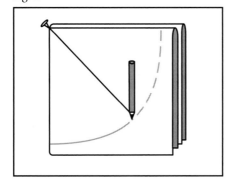

3. Use six strands of embroidery floss to baste 2" from edge around circle.
4. Place basket in center of fabric circle. Pull ends of floss to gather fabric around basket. Fill space between basket and fabric with desired amount of fiberfill. Pull ends of floss to tighten fabric around top of basket; knot ends together. Adjust gathers as necessary. Turn edges of fabric under; glue to rim of basket.
5. Place rubber band around basket 1½" below rim. Measure around basket; add 22". Cut one length from each ribbon the determined measurement. Knot ribbons over rubber band. Thread bell onto one ribbon end. Tie ribbon ends into a bow; notch ends.
6. Cut one 22" length from each ribbon. Tie ribbons into a bow. Cut three 6" lengths from star garland. Loosely wrap each length around pencil to curl; remove from pencil. Twist garland curls together at one end. Glue twisted ends to back of bow. Glue bow to basket; notch ends.
7. Arrange fabric in basket.

BUCKETFUL OF FUN

*W*hen it's raining buckets *outside, surprise a neighboring family with a pail full of snacks. Our nutty caramel popcorn is super easy to mix up using ready-made ice-cream topping. Select a galvanized bucket that's roomy enough for a bottle of soda and maybe a movie or two to pass the time away while skies are gray!*

EASY CARAMEL-NUT POPCORN

12 cups popped popcorn
 1 can (12 ounces) salted peanuts
 1 jar (12¼ ounces) caramel
      ice-cream topping

Preheat oven to 250 degrees. Combine popcorn and peanuts in a greased large roasting pan. Pour topping over mixture; stir until coated. Bake 1 hour, stirring every 15 minutes. Spread on greased aluminum foil to cool. Store in an airtight container.

Yield: about 11 cups popcorn

GALVANIZED BUCKET

You will need silver spray paint, galvanized bucket with handle (we used a 9⅝" dia. x 12"h bucket), hot glue gun, 32" of silver bead trim, and 1½ yds. of 2"w silver beaded wired organza ribbon. *For gift tag,* you will *also* need a black permanent fine-point marker, 2¾" square of white card stock, two 3" squares of ultra thin craft steel, stylus, ⅛" dia. hole punch, and silver braided cord.

1. Spray paint handle silver.
2. Glue trim around bucket. Tie ribbon into a bow around bucket; glue to secure.

3. For gift tag, use marker to write message on card stock; glue to one steel square. Use stylus to draw design and write message on remaining steel square; place on top of card stock-covered square. Punching through both layers of steel, punch hole in corner of tag. Use cord to attach tag to handle.

PARTY-SAURUS COOKIES

*M*ake a child's birthday party roar with these "dino-mite" favors. Sprinkled with color, our Spotted Dinosaur Cookies are delicious take-home treats. Pack several into wrapping paper-covered bags, complete with foam dinosaur magnets.

SPOTTED DINOSAUR COOKIES

- 3/4 cup butter or margarine, softened
- 1/2 cup confectioners sugar
- 1/2 cup firmly packed brown sugar
- 1 egg
- 1 teaspoon vanilla extract
- 2 1/2 cups all-purpose flour
- 1/4 teaspoon salt
- 5 teaspoons assorted colors of non-pareils

In a large bowl, cream butter and sugars until fluffy. Add egg and vanilla; beat until smooth. In a small bowl, combine flour and salt. Add dry ingredients to creamed mixture. Stir until a soft dough forms. Add non-pareils to dough; knead until well blended. Divide dough in half. Wrap in plastic wrap and chill 2 hours.

Preheat oven to 350 degrees. On a lightly floured surface, use a floured rolling pin to roll out dough to 1/8-inch thickness. Use a 4 x 2 1/2-inch dinosaur-shaped cookie cutter to cut out cookies. Transfer to a greased baking sheet. Bake 5 to 7 minutes or until bottoms are lightly browned. Transfer cookies to a wire rack to cool. Store in an airtight container.

Yield: about 3 1/2 dozen cookies

DINOSAUR BAGS

For each bag, you will need a dinosaur-shaped cookie cutter, craft foam in assorted colors, 1/8" dia. hole punch, craft glue, 3mm wiggle eye, 5/8" dia. magnet, lunch-size paper bag, wrapping paper, spray adhesive, 1/4" dia. hole punch, assorted colors of curling ribbon, and double-sided tape.

Use craft glue for all gluing unless otherwise indicated. Allow glue to dry after each application.

1. Draw around cookie cutter on craft foam; cut out. Use 1/8" dia. hole punch to punch dots from assorted colors of foam. Glue dots to body, eye to head, and magnet to back of dinosaur.

2. Draw around front of bag on wrapping paper; cut out 1/4" inside drawn lines. Apply spray adhesive to wrong side of paper; smooth over front of bag.

3. Place gift in bag. Fold top of bag 2" to front. Use 1/4" dia. hole punch to punch two holes 1" apart in center of folded portion of bag. Thread several strands of curling ribbon through holes in bag; knot ends at front of bag. Curl ribbon ends. Tape magnet to front of bag.

SPICY PECAN PAIL

EXTRA easy!

*T*hese fiery nuts will
leave 'em hankerin' for more!
Tex-Mex Pecans are coated
with spices and baked for range-
riding taste. Tie the nuts in a red
bandanna and deliver in a rope-
trimmed bucket with a sassy
boot-shaped gift tag.

TEX-MEX PECANS

3¹/₂ cups pecan halves (about
        14 ounces)
  1 tablespoon vegetable oil
  1 tablespoon ground cumin
  1 teaspoon chili powder
³/₄ teaspoon salt
¹/₈ teaspoon ground red pepper

Preheat oven to 300 degrees. Place
pecans in a lightly greased 9 x 13-inch
baking pan. In a small bowl, combine oil,
cumin, chili powder, salt, and red pepper.
Drizzle oil mixture over pecans; stir to
coat. Bake 25 minutes, stirring every
5 minutes. Spread on aluminum foil to
cool. Store in an airtight container.

Yield: about 4 cups pecans

BUCKET O' SPICY PECANS

You will need a bucket (we used a 5¹/₂"h
galvanized bucket), ³/₈" dia. rope,
hot glue gun, bandanna, and 20" of
jute twine.
For tag, you will *also* need photocopy of
tag design (page 111) on tan card stock,
colored pencils, and ¹/₈" dia. hole punch.

1. Measure around bucket. Cut a length of
rope the determined measurement. Glue
rope around bucket.

2. Line bucket with bandanna. Place gift
in bucket. Gather bandanna over gift. Tie
twine around gathers.

3. For tag, use pencils to color tag.
Leaving a ¹/₈" border, cut out tag. Punch
hole in boot loop. Tie one end of twine
through hole in tag; knot other end
of twine.

TEACHER'S TREAT

*E*verybody loves peanut butter, and this creamy dip gives a favorite teacher a rich way to enjoy it! Easy to make with only three ingredients, this delectable snack is great with apple slices. Pack the A+ present in a gift basket decorated with clever craft stick "pencils."

PEANUT BUTTER DIP

 1 package (8 ounces) cream cheese, softened
 1 jar (7 ounces) marshmallow creme
 1/4 cup smooth peanut butter
  Fresh fruit to serve

In a small bowl, combine cream cheese, marshmallow creme, and peanut butter. Beat at low speed of an electric mixer until smooth. Store in an airtight container in refrigerator. Serve at room temperature with fresh fruit.

Yield: about 1³/₄ cups dip

TEACHER'S BASKET

You will need utility scissors; two jumbo craft sticks; tracing paper; transfer paper; yellow, tan, and metallic silver acrylic paint; paintbrushes; black permanent fine-point marker; hot glue gun; a basket (we used a 9" x 11³/₄" x 5¹/₄"d wire basket); and fabric to line basket.
For jar lid cover, you will *also* need craft glue, jar with a 3¹/₄" dia. lid, and one 3¹/₈" dia. circle each of school-motif fabric and poster board.

1. Use utility scissors to cut one end of each craft stick to a point. Trace pencil design, page 111, onto tracing paper. Use transfer paper to transfer design to each craft stick. Follow *Painting Techniques,* page 122, to paint pencils.
3. Use marker to add details to pencils and write message on one pencil. Arrange and glue pencils to basket. Arrange fabric in basket.
4. For jar lid cover, use craft glue to glue fabric circle to poster board circle; allow to dry. Hot glue cover to top of lid.

HAPPY BIRTHDAY!

*F*or a delightfully different birthday confection, why not make a giant cookie and deliver it in a "lollipop" package! A fun way to celebrate for young and old alike, it's packed with goodies like candy-coated chocolate baking candies and crispy rice cereal. To keep the cookie fresh, wrap it with cellophane and tie off with colorful curling ribbon.

HAPPY BIRTHDAY COOKIE

COOKIE

- $1/3$ cup butter or margarine, softened
- $1/3$ cup granulated sugar
- $1/3$ cup firmly packed brown sugar
- 1 egg
- $1/4$ cup vegetable oil
- 1 teaspoon vanilla extract
- 1 cup plus 3 tablespoons all-purpose flour
- $1/2$ teaspoon baking soda
- $1/4$ teaspoon salt
- $2/3$ cup candy-coated chocolate mini baking candies, divided
- $1/3$ cup quick-cooking oats
- $1/3$ cup crispy rice cereal

ICING

- $1/2$ cup confectioners sugar
- 2 teaspoons cocoa
- 3 to 4 teaspoons milk
- $1/2$ teaspoon vanilla extract

Preheat oven to 325 degrees. For cookies, cream butter and sugars in a medium bowl until fluffy. Add egg, oil, and vanilla; beat until smooth. In a small bowl, combine flour, baking soda, and salt. Add dry ingredients to creamed mixture; stir until a soft dough forms. Stir in $1/3$ cup candies, oats, and cereal. Press dough into a greased 12-inch-diameter pizza pan. Sprinkle remaining $1/3$ cup candies on top of dough. Bake 23 to 25 minutes or until top is lightly browned. Transfer pan to a wire rack to cool completely.

For icing, combine confectioners sugar, cocoa, milk, and vanilla in a small bowl; stir until smooth. Transfer cooled cookie to a 12-inch-diameter cardboard cake board. Drizzle icing over cookie; let icing harden. Store in an airtight container.

Yield: about 12 servings

"HAPPY BIRTHDAY" LOLLIPOP AND TAG

You will need a hot glue gun, 20" of $3/8$" dia. dowel rod, cellophane, chenille stem, clear tape, and assorted curling ribbons.

For gift tag, you will *also* need tracing paper; card stock; red, green, and black permanent medium-point markers; and a hole punch.

1. For lollipop, glue dowel to back of cake board. Wrap cellophane around cookie and gather around dowel; secure with chenille stem. Use tape to secure sides of cellophane at back of lollipop.
2. Tie several lengths of ribbon into a bow around gathers; curl ribbon ends.
3. For tag, follow *Making Patterns,* page 122, to trace tag pattern, page 113, onto tracing paper; cut out. Use pattern to cut tag from card stock.
4. Use red marker to draw "stitches" along edges of tag. Use black marker to write message on tag and green marker to draw musical notes on tag.
5. Punch hole in tag; thread one streamer through hole and knot to secure.

HAVE A G-R-REAT DAY!

Creamy Coconut Candies are a "g-r-reat" pick-me-up for a friend who's facing a beastly schedule. Pack the bite-size squares in a window-topped box, then glue on an animal-print bow and a gilded gift tag.

COCONUT CANDIES

1¹/₂ cups granulated sugar
1¹/₂ cups firmly packed brown sugar
1¹/₂ cups whipping cream
¹/₂ cup cream of coconut
¹/₄ cup light corn syrup
¹/₈ teaspoon salt
¹/₄ cup butter or margarine
2 teaspoons vanilla extract
1 cup flaked coconut

Line a 9-inch square baking pan with aluminum foil, extending foil over 2 sides of pan; grease foil. Butter sides of a heavy Dutch oven. Combine sugars, whipping cream, cream of coconut, corn syrup, and salt in pan. Stirring constantly, cook over medium-low heat until sugar dissolves. Using a pastry brush dipped in hot water, wash down any sugar crystals on sides of pan. Attach a candy thermometer to pan, making sure thermometer does not touch bottom of pan. Increase heat to medium and bring to a boil. Cook, without stirring, until mixture reaches soft-ball stage (approximately 234 to 240 degrees). Test about ¹/₂ teaspoon mixture in ice water. Mixture will easily form a ball in ice water but will flatten when removed from water. Remove from heat and place pan in 2 inches of cold water in sink. Add butter and vanilla; do not stir. Cool to approximately 110 degrees. Remove from sink. Using medium speed of an electric

mixer, beat until candy thickens and begins to lose its gloss. Stir in coconut. Pour into prepared pan. Cool completely. Cut into 1-inch squares. Store in an airtight container in refrigerator.

Yield: about 5 dozen pieces candy

"G-R-REAT" GIFT TOPPER

You will need 22" of 1¹/₄"w animal-motif wired ribbon, button, card stock, gold paint pen, ¹/₈" dia. hole punch, and 7" of gold cord.

1. Tie ribbon into a bow; glue button to knot of bow.
2. Cut a four-sided shape from card stock (ours measures 3¹/₂" along bottom and 2¹/₂" along top). Use paint pen to write message and draw border on tag.
3. Punch hole in tag. Use cord to attach tag to bow.

68

SWEET INDULGENCE

*T*his fudge-filled volume is a deliciously novel gift for your fellow book club members. Create a "classic" container by simply embellishing a papier-mâché book box with wrapping paper. Tuck in morsels of Chocolate Swirl Fudge and watch the plot thicken — the group will savor the happy ending!

CHOCOLATE SWIRL FUDGE

- 1/4 cup semisweet chocolate chips
- 1 teaspoon vegetable shortening
- 3 cups sugar
- 1 cup whipping cream
- 1/2 cup butter or margarine
- 1/8 teaspoon salt
- 1 package (10 1/2 ounces) miniature marshmallows
- 1 package (6 ounces) white baking chocolate, chopped
- 6 ounces vanilla candy coating, chopped
- 1 teaspoon vanilla extract

Line a 9 x 13-inch baking pan with aluminum foil, extending foil over ends of pan; grease foil. In top of a double boiler, combine chocolate chips and shortening over hot, not simmering, water; stir until mixture melts. Turn off heat.

Butter sides of a heavy large saucepan. Combine sugar, whipping cream, butter, and salt in saucepan. Attach a candy thermometer to pan, making sure thermometer does not touch bottom of pan. Stirring constantly, bring to a boil over medium heat. Cook, stirring constantly, until mixture reaches 234 degrees (about 5 minutes). Remove from heat. Add marshmallows, white

chocolate, and candy coating; stir until melted. Stir in vanilla. Pour into prepared pan. Drizzle melted chocolate mixture over fudge. Using tip of a knife, gently swirl chocolate into fudge. Chill 1 hour or until firm. Use ends of foil to lift fudge from pan. Cut into 1-inch squares. Store in an airtight container in refrigerator.

Yield: about 8 dozen pieces fudge

COVERED BOOK BOX

You will need a 5"w x 7 1/2"h x 2 1/2"d papier-mâché book-shaped box, wrapping paper, spray adhesive, gold acrylic paint, paintbrush, photocopy of label (page 112) on card stock, coordinating color of card stock for border, gold paint pen, and wood-tone spray.

Throughout these instructions, we refer to the book box as "book."

1. Use acrylic paint to lightly paint page edges of book gold.
2. For book cover, cut a 7 1/2" x 12 3/4" piece from wrapping paper. Apply spray adhesive to wrong side of paper. Matching edges, smooth paper around book.
3. For book label, use paint pen to paint over corners and outlines of photocopy. Trim photocopy to 1/16" around label. Apply spray adhesive to wrong side of label; glue to card stock for border. Leaving a 1/8" border, cut out label. Lightly spray label with wood-tone spray; allow to dry. Apply spray adhesive to wrong side of label; glue to front of book.

GOOD-NEIGHBOR CAKES

*T*he tangy flavor of these moist cakes gets a boost from a "secret" ingredient — baby food! Apricot-Nut Cakes make great neighborhood gifts when they're packaged in market baskets accented with fruit and lined with vibrant fabric.

APRICOT-NUT CAKES

- 1 package (18¼ ounces) yellow cake mix
- 4 eggs
- ¾ cup apricot nectar
- ¾ cup vegetable oil
- 1 jar (4 ounces) apricot baby food
- 1 cup finely chopped pecans, toasted
- 1 cup confectioners sugar
- ¼ cup apricot brandy
- 4 teaspoons freshly squeezed lemon juice

Preheat oven to 325 degrees. Grease three 3½ x 7½-inch loaf pans, line bottoms with waxed paper; grease waxed paper. In a large bowl, combine cake mix, eggs, apricot nectar, oil, and baby food; beat until well blended. Stir in pecans. Pour batter into prepared pans. Bake 40 to 45 minutes or until a toothpick inserted in center of cake comes out clean. Cool in pans 10 minutes on a wire rack. Remove from pans and place on a wire rack with waxed paper underneath.

In a small bowl, combine confectioners sugar, brandy, and lemon juice; stir until smooth. Spoon glaze over warm cakes. Allow cakes to cool completely. Store in an airtight container in refrigerator.

Yield: 3 small cakes

MARKET BASKETS

For each basket, you will need a 6½" x 8¼" market basket with a ⅞"w handle, ⅞"w and ¼"w grosgrain ribbons, hot glue gun, artificial greenery (we used a stem of leaves with berries), and fabric to line basket.

For gift tag, you will *also* need craft glue, 1½" x 2⅜" piece of fabric, 1½" x 2⅜" and 1¼" x 2" pieces of light-colored card stock, and a black permanent fine-point marker.

Use hot glue for all gluing unless otherwise indicated.

1. Measure handle of basket; add ½". Cut one piece from each ribbon the determined measurement. Center and glue ⅞"w ribbon, then ¼"w ribbon along handle.
2. Glue stem of greenery at base of handle.
3. Measure around rim of basket; add ½". Cut one piece from each ribbon the determined measurement. Overlapping ends at back, glue ⅞"w ribbon, then ¼"w ribbon around rim of basket.
4. Arrange fabric in basket. Tie ¼"w ribbon into a bow around wrapped cake. Place cake in basket.
5. For tag, use craft glue to glue fabric piece to 1½" x 2⅜" piece of card stock. Use marker to write message on 1¼" x 2" piece of card stock; center and glue to fabric side of tag.

AUTUMN MACAROONS

A batch of light, crispy Maple-Nut Macaroons makes a super gift for a housewarming party or back-to-school treat. Pack the tasty morsels in a fabric-covered Shaker box decorated with autumn leaf appliqués and a ribbon bow for a charming fall project.

MAPLE-NUT MACAROONS

- 3 egg whites
- 1/2 teaspoon cream of tartar
- 3/4 cup plus 2 tablespoons sugar
- 2 cups chopped pecans, toasted and finely ground
- 2 tablespoons maple syrup
- 1 teaspoon vanilla extract

Preheat oven to 300 degrees. In a medium bowl, beat egg whites and cream of tartar until foamy. Gradually add sugar, beating until stiff peaks form. Fold in pecans, maple syrup, and vanilla. Drop by rounded teaspoonfuls onto a baking sheet lined with parchment paper. Bake 15 to 18 minutes or until bottoms are lightly browned. Transfer cookies to a wire rack to cool. Store in an airtight container.

Yield: about 6 dozen cookies

FALL SHAKER BOX

You will need an oval papier-mâché Shaker box (we used a 7³/8"w x 10"h x 5"d box), paper-backed fusible web, fabric to cover box lid, hot glue gun, fabrics for appliqués, brown permanent fine-point marker, and 1"w grosgrain ribbon.

1. Draw around lid on paper side of web. Cut out along drawn line. Fuse web to wrong side of fabric. Cut out fabric 3/4" outside edge of web. Clip edges at 1/2" intervals to 1/4" from web. Center and fuse fabric to lid; glue clipped edges to side of lid.

2. Use patterns, page 112, and follow *Making Appliqués*, page 122, to make one each of stems A, B, and C; one large leaf; and two small leaf appliqués.

3. Arrange appliqués on lid; fuse in place.

4. Use marker to draw details on leaves.

5. Measure around lid; add 1/2". Cut two lengths of ribbon the determined measurement. Covering raw edge of fabric and overlapping ends at back, glue one ribbon around bottom edge of lid and second ribbon around bottom edge of box.

6. Cut a 12" length of ribbon; tie into a bow. Glue bow to front of box lid.

*T*his clever canister holds the secret to a great gift — it's filled with tasty Quick Oatmeal Muffin Mix! A round oatmeal box is dressed up like a chef to make the cute container. Your friends will love starting their day with this wholesome breakfast that's so easy to bake. To give them an instant start, include a batch of fresh-baked muffins.

QUICK OATMEAL MUFFIN MIX

- 4 cups all-purpose flour
- 1³/4 cups sugar
- ¹/2 cup dried buttermilk powder
- 1¹/2 tablespoons baking powder
- 1 teaspoon salt
- 1 teaspoon ground cinnamon
- ¹/2 teaspoon ground nutmeg
- 4 packets (about 1.2 ounces each) fruit and cream instant oatmeal (we used peaches and cream)
- 1¹/4 cups chilled butter or margarine, cut into pieces

In a large bowl, combine flour, sugar, buttermilk powder, baking powder, salt, cinnamon, and nutmeg. Stir in instant oatmeal mix. With a pastry blender or 2 knives, cut in butter until mixture resembles coarse meal. Divide mix into 2 resealable plastic bags (about 5¹/2 cups mix in each bag). Store in refrigerator. Give each bag of mix with baking instructions.

Yield: about 11 cups muffin mix

To bake: Store muffin mix in refrigerator until ready to bake. Preheat oven to 400 degrees. In a medium bowl, combine bag of muffin mix, 1 cup water, and 1 beaten egg; stir just until moistened. Fill greased muffin cups about three-fourths full. Bake 15 to 20 minutes or until edges are lightly browned and a toothpick inserted in center of muffin comes out clean. Serve warm.

Yield: about 1 dozen muffins

"CHEF'S SECRET" CANISTER

You will need a round oatmeal canister with lid; white, tan, and brown craft foam; clear Con-Tact® paper; ruler; craft knife and cutting mat; low melt glue gun; fiberfill; drawing compass; decorative-edge craft scissors; fabric to cover canister; spray adhesive; tracing paper; white acrylic paint; paintbrush; black permanent medium-point marker; and 14" of 1"w grosgrain ribbon.

1. For hat, measure around lid of canister. Cut one piece each from white craft foam and Con-Tact® paper 3" by the determined measurement. Apply plastic to one side of foam. Place foam plastic side down on cutting mat. Beginning at one short end, use ruler and craft knife to carefully score foam at ¹/2" intervals. Overlapping short ends at back and matching bottom edges, glue hat around lid of canister. Fill hat with fiberfill. Use compass to draw a 5¹/2" dia. circle on white foam. Use craft scissors to cut out circle; glue to top of hat.

2. Measure height of canister. Measure around canister; add ¹/2". Cut a piece of fabric the determined measurements. Apply spray adhesive to wrong side of fabric. Overlapping edges at back, smooth fabric around canister.

3. Trace patterns, page 113, onto tracing paper. Use patterns to cut one face and two eyelids from tan foam; two eyebrows, two eyes, and one mustache from white foam; and two pupils from brown foam. Overlapping as necessary, glue shapes to face. Paint white highlights on pupils. Use marker to draw nose and mouth on face.

4. Place hat on canister. Aligning top of face with bottom edge of hat, glue face to canister.

5. For bow tie, tie ribbon into a bow and glue to canister.

HOMESTYLE TASTE

*W*e all scream for
*ice cream, especially when
it's crowned with spirited Apple-
Rum-Raisin Sauce. It's a delicious
feature for an old-fashioned ice-
cream social. Present a jar of
the topping along with a cross-
stitched apron to bring out
real homemade style.*

APPLE-RUM-RAISIN SAUCE

- ½ cup golden raisins
- ¼ cup plus 2 tablespoons dark rum
- 4 cups peeled, cored, and sliced
  Granny Smith apples (about
  4 large apples)
- 1 cup firmly packed brown sugar
- ½ cup water
- 2 tablespoons freshly squeezed
  lemon juice
- 1 teaspoon grated lemon zest

In a small microwave-safe bowl,
combine raisins and rum. Microwave on
high power (100%) 1 minute or until
mixture is heated through. Cover and
set aside.

In a heavy large saucepan, combine
apples, brown sugar, water, lemon juice,
and lemon zest. Stirring frequently, bring
to a boil over medium heat. Reduce heat
to medium-low. Cover and simmer
15 minutes or until apples are tender.
Uncover and cook about 10 minutes
longer or until liquid is a thick syrup.
Remove from heat. Mash apples; stir in
raisin mixture. Serve at room temperature
over ice cream or cake. Store in an
airtight container in refrigerator.

Yield: about 3 cups sauce

APRON

You will need three 6" squares each of
waste canvas and non-fusible interfacing,
masking tape; three-pocket chef's apron,
embroidery floss (see color key,
page 114), sharp needle, and tweezers.
For jar lid cover, you will *also* need a jar
with lid, fabric, and raffia.

*Refer to Cross Stitch, page 123, before
beginning project.*

1. Using three strands of floss for *Cross
Stitch* and one strand for *Backstitch*,
center and stitch one design, page 114,
on each pocket.
2. For jar lid cover, draw around lid on
wrong side of fabric. Cut out circle 2"
outside drawn line. Center fabric circle
over jar lid; secure with rubber band.
Knot several strands of raffia around lid.

WELCOME, NEIGHBOR!

Give a warm welcome to the "new kids on the block" with a creamy Peanut Butter Cake! Thick, delicious icing makes the dessert absolutely mouth-watering. A hand-tinted tag and a big plaid bow tie up the cake carrier with homey goodness.

PEANUT BUTTER CAKE

An aluminum foil cake pan with plastic lid makes this cake easy to give.

CAKE

- 1 package (18½ ounces) butter-recipe yellow cake mix
- 1 container (8 ounces) sour cream
- ⅓ cup vegetable oil
- ⅓ cup smooth peanut butter
- 3 eggs, separated
- 1 teaspoon vanilla extract

ICING

- ¼ cup smooth peanut butter
- 2 tablespoons butter or margarine, softened
- 1 teaspoon vanilla extract
- 3 cups confectioners sugar
- 4 to 5 tablespoons milk

Preheat oven to 350 degrees. For cake, combine cake mix, sour cream, oil, peanut butter, egg yolks, and vanilla in a large bowl; beat until well blended. In a small bowl, beat egg whites until stiff; fold into batter. Pour batter into a greased 9 x 13-inch aluminum foil baking pan. Bake 30 to 35 minutes or until a toothpick inserted in center of cake comes out clean. Allow cake to cool completely.

For icing, combine peanut butter, butter, and vanilla in a medium bowl; beat until smooth. Add confectioners sugar and

gradually add milk; beat until smooth. Ice top of cake. Cover with lid.

Yield: 12 to 15 servings

"WARM WELCOME" TAG

You will need craft glue, 2¾" x 5" piece each of fabric and poster board, colored pencils, photocopy of tag design (page 113), and decorative-edge craft scissors.

1. Glue fabric to poster board; allow to dry.
2. Use colored pencils to color tag. Use craft scissors to cut out tag. Center and glue to fabric side of poster board.

75

BEWITCHING BROWNIES

Want to offer something different to trick-or-treaters this year? Try delicious Pumpkin Brownies flavored with pumpkin pie spice. Bewitching pins created from craft foam and colored raffia are a great way to wrap up the spooky snacks. They're sure to leave your Halloween guests "howling" for more!

PUMPKIN BROWNIES

BROWNIES

    3/4 cup butter or margarine, softened
    3/4 cup firmly packed brown sugar
    3/4 cup granulated sugar
    1 teaspoon vanilla extract
    1 cup canned pumpkin
    2 eggs
 1 1/2 cups all-purpose flour
    1/2 cup cocoa
    2 teaspoons baking powder
    3/4 teaspoon pumpkin pie spice
    1/4 teaspoon salt

ICING

    4 cups confectioners sugar
    1/3 cup cocoa
    1/3 cup butter or margarine, softened
    1/4 cup boiling water
    1 teaspoon vanilla extract

Preheat oven to 350 degrees. For brownies, cream butter, sugars, and vanilla in a large bowl until fluffy. Beat in pumpkin and eggs until smooth. In a small bowl, combine flour, cocoa, baking powder, pumpkin pie spice, and salt. Gradually add dry ingredients to creamed mixture; beat until well blended. Spread batter into a greased 10 1/2 x 15 1/2-inch jellyroll pan. Bake 14 to 16 minutes or

until a toothpick inserted in center of brownies comes out with a few crumbs clinging to it. Cool in pan on a wire rack.

For icing, combine confectioners sugar and cocoa in a medium bowl. Add butter, water, and vanilla; beat until smooth. Spread icing on brownies. Cut into 2-inch squares. Store in an airtight container.

Yield: about 3 dozen brownies

WITCHY PINS AND GIFT TAGS

For each pin, you will need tracing paper; green and black craft foam; decorative-edge craft scissors; transfer paper; white, light green, green, and black acrylic paint; paintbrushes; black permanent fine-point and medium-point markers; toothpick; orange raffia; low temperature glue gun; craft knife and cutting mat; pin back; cellophane bag; and a 1 1/4" x 22" torn fabric strip.

For gift tag, you will *also* need tan card stock, hole punch, and 6" of 1/16"w orange satin ribbon.

Refer to Painting Techniques, page 122, for painting tips.

1. Trace patterns, this page, onto tracing paper; cut out. Use patterns to cut hat and hat brim from black craft foam. Use craft scissors and patterns to cut head and nose from green craft foam.

2. Use transfer paper to transfer face to head. Paint eyes white, pupils black, and lips light green. Use fine-point marker to draw over transferred lines. Use end of toothpick to paint green dots on face for freckles and white dots on pupils for highlights. Glue nose to face and hat to head.

3. Cut several 8" lengths of raffia; glue to front and back of head for hair.

4. Use craft knife to make cut in hat brim as indicated on pattern. Insert top of hat into opening in hat brim; glue to secure. Glue pin back to back of witch.

5. For gift tag, use craft scissors to cut a 2" x 6" piece from card stock. Use medium-point marker to write message on bottom half of tag. Gently press pin back on tag to mark placement for holes. Punch a hole at each mark and at top of tag. Thread ribbon through top hole; knot ends together for hanger. Pin witch to tag through remaining holes.

6. Place gift in bag. Thread fabric strip through hanger of tag; tie strip into a bow around top of bag.

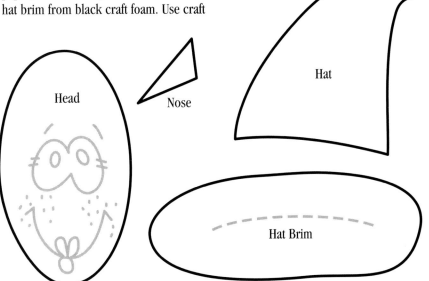

Head

Nose

Hat

Hat Brim

JALAPEÑO BOO BRITTLE

This nutty candy may appear innocent enough, but it packs a peppery twist! Made with bits of pickled jalapeños, our peanut brittle is a fun treat for Halloween. For an extra-spooky touch, package it in a ghostly gift bag.

JALAPEÑO-PEANUT BRITTLE

1½ cups sugar
½ cup light corn syrup
¼ cup water
1 package (12 ounces) raw Spanish peanuts
¼ cup chopped pickled jalapeño peppers
1½ tablespoons butter or margarine
½ teaspoon salt
1 teaspoon baking soda
¼ teaspoon green paste food coloring

Butter sides of a heavy large saucepan. Combine sugar, corn syrup, and water in saucepan. Stirring constantly, cook over medium-low heat until sugar dissolves. Using a pastry brush dipped in hot water, wash down any sugar crystals on sides of pan. Attach a candy thermometer to pan, making sure thermometer does not touch bottom of pan. Increase heat to medium and bring to a boil. Cook, without stirring, until mixture reaches 230 degrees (about 3 minutes). Stir in peanuts and peppers. Stirring occasionally, continue to cook until mixture reaches hard-crack stage (300 to 310 degrees) and turns golden brown. Test about ½ teaspoon mixture in ice water. Mixture will form brittle threads in ice water and will remain brittle when removed from water. Remove from heat. Stir in butter, salt, and baking soda

(mixture will foam); stir until butter melts. Stir in food coloring. Pour mixture onto greased heavy-duty aluminum foil. Placing 1 rubber spatula on top and a second spatula underneath, lift edges of brittle and stretch as brittle cools. Cool completely; break into pieces. Store in an airtight container.

Yield: about 1 pound, 9 ounces candy

GHOSTLY TREAT BAG

You will need tracing paper; white poster board; black permanent fine-point marker; hot glue gun; 3½" wooden craft pick; lunch-size paper bag; orange tissue paper; white and black checked tissue paper; and orange, purple, and black curling ribbon.

1. Trace patterns, page 115, onto tracing paper; cut out. Use patterns to cut one each of ghost, small tag, and large tag from poster board.
2. Use marker to draw eyes on ghost and to write messages on tags. Glue small tag to one end of craft pick; glue remaining end to back of ghost's hand.
3. Line bag with tissue paper; place gift in bag. Tie ribbons into a bow around bag; curl ends.
4. Glue ghost and large tag to bag.

BOO BITES

These creepy cookies are a hauntingly good treat! Made using a simple recipe, the glazed cookies are fun and easy to decorate. Tuck them in a "boo-tiful" cross-stitched tote for delivering happy Halloween wishes!

GHOST COOKIES

COOKIES

¹/₂	cup butter or margarine, softened
³/₄	cup granulated sugar
¹/₄	cup firmly packed brown sugar
¹/₄	cup milk
1	egg
1¹/₂	teaspoons vanilla extract
2	cups all-purpose flour
¹/₂	teaspoon baking powder
¹/₂	teaspoon salt

ICING

5	cups confectioners sugar
6 to 7	tablespoons water
1	tablespoon light corn syrup
1	teaspoon vanilla extract
1	tube (4¹/₄ ounces) black decorating icing
1	tube (4¹/₄ ounces) orange decorating icing

For cookies, trace pattern, page 116, onto stencil plastic; cut out. In a medium bowl, cream butter and sugars until fluffy. Add milk, egg, and vanilla; beat until smooth. In a small bowl, combine flour, baking powder, and salt. Add dry ingredients to creamed mixture; stir until well blended. Divide dough into thirds. Wrap in plastic wrap and chill 2 hours.

Preheat oven to 400 degrees. On a lightly floured surface, use a floured rolling pin to roll out one third of dough to slightly less than ¹/₄-inch thickness. Use

pattern to cut out cookies. Place 1 inch apart on a lightly greased baking sheet. Bake 5 to 7 minutes or until bottoms are lightly browned. Transfer cookies to a wire rack with waxed paper underneath to cool. Repeat with remaining dough.

For icing, combine confectioners sugar, water, corn syrup, and vanilla in a large bowl; stir until smooth. Spoon icing over cookies; let icing harden.

To decorate cookies, transfer black and orange icing to pastry bags fitted with small round tips. Use black to pipe eyes, nose, and mouth onto each cookie. Use orange to pipe bow onto each cookie. Store in a single layer in an airtight container.

Yield: about 14 cookies

MINI-TOTE

You will need embroidery floss (see color key, page 116), Lil' Tote (14 ct), tissue paper, and assorted curling ribbon.

Refer to Cross Stitch, page 123, before beginning project.

1. Using three strands of floss for *Cross Stitch* and one strand for *Backstitch*, center and stitch design, page 116, on tote.
2. Line tote with tissue paper. Place gift in tote. Tie curling ribbon into a bow around handles; curl ribbon ends.

GOBLIN SNACKS

Filled with Goblin Snack Mix, these "batty" bags will be a monster-size hit at the school Halloween party! The sweet, crunchy-munchy mix is super simple to toss together.

GOBLIN SNACK MIX

2 packages (7¹/₂ ounces each) chocolate-covered pretzels
1 package (8¹/₂ ounces) mini chocolate chip cookies
1 package (16 ounces) candy-coated peanut butter pieces
2 cups small orange slice candies

In a large bowl, combine pretzels, cookies, peanut butter pieces, and orange slice candies. Store in an airtight container.

Yield: about 13 cups candy

"BATTY" TREAT BAGS

For each bag, you will need tracing paper, black poster board, black glossy gift bag (we used a 4¹/₄" x 7¹/₂" bag), hot glue gun, black chenille stem, two 10mm wiggle eyes, and yellow and orange curling ribbon.

1. Follow *Making Patterns*, page 122, and trace wings pattern, page 115, onto tracing paper; cut out. Use pattern to cut wings from poster board.
2. Place gift in bag. Fold top of bag ¹/₂" to front twice; glue center of fold to secure.
3. Bend chenille stem to form handle; center and glue ends to back of bag. Glue wings to back of bag and eyes to front of bag.
4. Knot several lengths of ribbon around handle; curl ribbon ends.

ALWAYS IN SEASON

Like a treasured friendship, our Year-Round Apricot Jam is always in season! Dried fruit and canned nectar are used to make this sweet condiment that's delicious atop fluffy biscuits. Invite someone special over for breakfast, then send home a jar of the jam in a patchwork bag that celebrates your friendship.

YEAR-ROUND APRICOT JAM

- 4 cups sugar
- 1 can (11½ ounces) apricot nectar
- 2 packages (6 ounces each) dried apricots, chopped
- ½ cup water
- ¼ cup freshly squeezed lemon juice
- 1 pouch (3 ounces) liquid fruit pectin

In a heavy large saucepan, combine sugar, apricot nectar, apricots, water, and lemon juice until well blended. Stirring constantly over high heat, bring mixture to a rolling boil. Stir in liquid pectin. Stirring constantly, bring to a rolling boil again and boil 1 minute. Remove from heat; skim off foam and let stand 20 minutes. Spoon jam into heat-resistant jars; cover and cool to room temperature. Store in refrigerator.

Yield: about 5½ cups jam

CANVAS TOTE BAG

You will need paper-backed fusible web, three coordinating fabrics, small canvas tote bag with handles (we used a 7" square bag), black permanent fine-point marker, craft glue, and tissue paper.

1. Follow *Making Appliqués*, page 122, to make one 4½" square background from first fabric, two 1½" squares from second fabric, and two 1" squares from third fabric. Do not remove paper backing from background. Cut 1" and 1½" squares in half diagonally.
2. Arrange triangles on background; fuse in place. Using tips of triangles as a guide, cut corners of background (Fig. 1). Remove paper backing from background and position design on bag (Fig. 2) fuse in place.

Fig. 1   Fig. 2

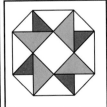

3. Use marker to draw "stitches" and write message around design.
4. Tear a 1" x 32" strip from one fabric. Matching long edges, fold strip in half. Tie strip into a bow around bag; glue to secure.
5. Place gift, then tissue paper in bag.

*F*olks can gobble up our *Apple Pie Squares without feeling guilty! These indulgent snacks are low in fat, but high in flavor. Package the sweet surprises in a fabric-covered "gobbler" box tied with warm plaid ribbon.*

APPLE PIE SQUARES

CAKE

 2 cups all-purpose flour
 2 cups sugar
 1 teaspoon baking soda
 1 teaspoon apple pie spice
 1/2 teaspoon salt
 1 can (21 ounces) apple pie filling
 1/2 cup nonfat egg substitute
 1 teaspoon vanilla extract
   Vegetable cooking spray

GLAZE

 1/2 cup firmly packed brown sugar
 1/4 cup apple juice
 1/2 cup confectioners sugar
 1/2 teaspoon vanilla extract
 1/8 teaspoon salt

Preheat oven to 350 degrees. For cake, combine flour, sugar, baking soda, apple pie spice, and salt in a large bowl. Add pie filling, egg substitute, and vanilla; beat just until blended and apples are coarsely chopped. Spread batter into a 9 x 13-inch baking pan lightly sprayed with cooking spray. Bake 30 to 35 minutes or until a toothpick inserted in center of cake comes out clean and top is golden brown. Cool in pan.

For glaze, combine brown sugar and apple juice in a small saucepan. Stirring constantly, bring to a boil over medium-high heat; boil 2 minutes. Pour mixture into a heatproof medium bowl. Add confectioners sugar, vanilla, and salt; beat until smooth. Pour glaze over cake. Let glaze harden. Cut into 2-inch squares. Store in an airtight container.

Yield: 2 dozen squares

1 serving (1 square): 159 calories, 0.3 gram fat, 1.8 grams protein, 38.1 grams carbohydrate

APPLE PIE "GOBBLER" BOX

You will need box with lid (we used an 11" square x 1³/₄"d papier-mâché box); fabric to cover lid of box; ruler; spray adhesive; 2¹/₃ yds. of 1³/₈"w coordinating ribbon; hot glue gun; 4" of floral wire; tracing paper; transfer paper; tan and brown craft foam; black permanent medium-point marker; white, yellow, and orange acrylic paint; paintbrushes; and decorative-edge craft scissors.

1. Measure width and length of lid including sides; add 1" to each measurement. Cut a piece of fabric the determined measurement. Center lid on wrong side of fabric and draw around lid.
2. Measure height of side of lid. Use ruler to draw lines the determined measurement outside drawn lines, extending lines to edges of fabric. Draw diagonal lines from corners of outer lines to corners of original lines.
3. Cut away outer corners of fabric and clip along diagonal lines (Fig. 1).

Fig. 1

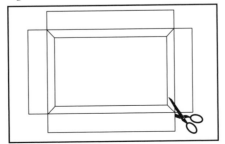

4. Apply spray adhesive to wrong side of fabric. Center lid top side down on fabric, matching lid to original drawn lines.
5. Smooth fabric onto front and back sides of lid. Smooth excess fabric around corners onto adjacent sides and to inside of lid, clipping as necessary (Fig. 2).

Fig. 2

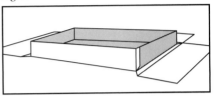

6. To cover each end, smooth fabric onto ends of lid. Carefully trim excess fabric even with corners. Smooth fabric to inside of lid.
7. Measure across lid, including sides; add 1". Cut a length of ribbon the determined measurement. Centering ribbon across top of lid, glue ribbon ends to inside of lid. Follow *Making a Bow*, page 121, to make a bow with eight 6" loops and two 4" streamers. Center and glue bow to top of lid.
8. Trace patterns, page 117, onto tracing paper. Use transfer paper to transfer turkey, wing A, and wing B designs to brown craft foam; cut out along outer lines. Paint eye white, beak and feet yellow, and wattle orange. Use marker to outline and add details to turkey and wings.
9. For tag, use craft scissors to cut a 2" x 3" piece from tan foam. Glue wings to top corners of tag. Use marker to write message on tag. Glue tag to turkey. Glue turkey to bow.

COOKIE BASKET

*C*ookies, cookies, and more cookies — this easy recipe makes a lot! Nutty brickle chips and toasted almonds give *Toffee Almond Cookies* a little something extra. A cute cross-stitched basket liner announces your tasty gift with style.

TOFFEE ALMOND COOKIES

- 1 cup butter or margarine, softened
- 2 cups firmly packed brown sugar
- 2 eggs
- 1 teaspoon almond extract
- 1 teaspoon vanilla extract
- 3 cups all-purpose flour
- 1 teaspoon baking powder
- 1/2 teaspoon salt
- 1 package (7 1/2 ounces) almond brickle chips
- 1 cup slivered almonds, toasted

Preheat oven to 350 degrees. In a large bowl, cream butter and brown sugar until fluffy. Add eggs and extracts; beat until smooth. In a medium bowl, combine flour, baking powder, and salt. Add dry ingredients to creamed mixture; beat until well blended. Stir in brickle chips and almonds. Drop by heaping teaspoonfuls onto a greased baking sheet. Bake 8 to 10 minutes or until bottoms are lightly browned. Transfer cookies to a wire rack to cool. Store in an airtight container.

Yield: about 7 dozen cookies

COOKIE BASKET

You will need embroidery floss (see color key, page 118), an Ivory Sal-Em™ Cloth Bread Cover (14 ct), basket (we

used a 7" dia. basket with handle), and 25" of 2"w wired ribbon.

Refer to Cross Stitch, page 123, before beginning project.

1. Using three strands of floss for *Cross Stitch* and one strand for *Backstitch* and *French Knots*, stitch design, page 118, on one corner of bread cover 3/4" from outer edge of fringe.

2. Place liner in basket. Tie ribbon into a bow around handle.

COOKIES ON THE SPOT

*Y*ou'll always be ready to present an impromptu gift when you keep ready-to-bake rolls of homemade Chocolate-Peanut Butter Cookie dough in your freezer. For delivery, slip the rolls into neat fabric tubes that you whipped up ahead of time. The baking instructions are written on a fun cookie-shaped tag.

CHOCOLATE-PEANUT BUTTER COOKIES

This cookie dough can be made ahead and frozen.

1/2	cup butter or margarine, softened
1/2	cup crunchy peanut butter
1/2	cup firmly packed brown sugar
1/2	cup granulated sugar
1	egg
1	teaspoon vanilla extract
1²/₃	cups all-purpose flour
1/2	teaspoon baking powder
1/4	teaspoon salt
1	cup semisweet chocolate mini chips

In a large bowl, cream butter, peanut butter, and sugars until fluffy. Add egg and vanilla; beat until smooth. In a small bowl, combine flour, baking powder, and salt. Add dry ingredients to creamed mixture; stir until a soft dough forms. Stir in chocolate chips. Divide dough into thirds. Shape each third into a 7-inch-long roll. Wrap in plastic wrap. Store in freezer. Give with baking instructions.

Yield: 3 rolls cookie dough

To bake: Preheat oven to 375 degrees. Let dough stand at room temperature 15 minutes. With a serrated knife, cut dough into 1/4-inch slices. Place on an ungreased baking sheet. Bake 7 to 9 minutes or until bottoms are golden brown. Transfer to a wire rack to cool. Store in an airtight container.

Yield: about 2 dozen cookies per roll

FABRIC TUBES WITH "COOKIE" TAGS

For each tube, you will need a 6" x 15" piece of fabric, pinking shears, and two 22" lengths of 1/4"w grosgrain ribbon.

For each tag, you will *also* need tracing paper; tan, brown, and dark brown fabric scraps; paper-backed fusible web; craft glue; poster board; hole punch; 6" of floss; and a black permanent fine-point marker.

1. For tube, matching right sides and long edges and using a 1/4" seam allowance, sew long edges of fabric together to form a tube. Turn right side out. Use pinking shears to trim ends. Place wrapped cookie dough roll in tube. Tie ribbon into a bow around each end.

2. For tag, use pattern, page 117, and follow *Making Appliqués*, page 122, to make one cookie appliqué each from tan and brown fabric. Fuse brown cookie to poster board. Cut poster board even with edge of fabric. Trim 1/4" from edge of tan cookie; fuse to center of brown cookie. For "chips," snip several four-sided pieces from dark brown fabric; glue to tan cookie. Punch hole in tag. Use marker to write baking instructions on back of tag. Use floss to attach tag to tube.

THANKSGIVING LOAF

Happy Thanksgiving

Chock-full of fruit and nuts, our spicy Apple-Cranberry-Nut Bread is a great way to enjoy the glorious days of autumn. To share the goodness at Thanksgiving, fashion a quick-to-stitch felt bag embellished with leaf appliqués.

APPLE-CRANBERRY-NUT BREAD

    1   medium baking apple, peeled,
          cored, and cut into pieces
          (about 1¹/₂ cups)
    1   cup fresh cranberries
    2   cups all-purpose flour
    1   cup sugar
    2   teaspoons baking powder
  ¹/₂   teaspoon baking soda
  ¹/₂   teaspoon salt
  ¹/₂   teaspoon apple pie spice
  ¹/₂   cup orange juice
  ¹/₄   cup vegetable oil
    1   egg
    1   teaspoon grated orange zest
    1   teaspoon vanilla extract
    1   cup chopped pecans

Preheat oven to 350 degrees. Grease a 5 x 9-inch loaf pan and line with waxed paper. Process apple pieces and cranberries in a food processor until coarsely chopped. In a large bowl, combine flour, sugar, baking powder, baking soda, salt, and apple pie spice. In a small bowl, combine orange juice, oil, egg, orange zest, and vanilla. Stir orange juice mixture, apple mixture, and pecans into dry ingredients just until blended. Spoon batter into prepared pan. Bake 55 to 60 minutes or until a toothpick inserted in center of bread comes out clean and top is golden brown. Cool in pan 10 minutes. Remove from pan and cool completely on a wire rack. Store in an airtight container.

Yield: 1 loaf bread

AUTUMN BAG

You will need an 11" x 36" piece of tan felt; tracing paper; green, brown, dark brown, and black felt scraps; green and black embroidery floss; and a ¹/₂" x 22" strip of brown felt.
For tag, you will *also* need tan card stock, craft glue, and a black permanent medium-point marker.

Use three strands of black floss and follow Embroidery Stitches, page 123, for all embroidery unless otherwise indicated.

1. Matching right sides and short edges, fold tan felt in half; press. Use a ¹/₂" seam allowance to sew sides of bag. For each bottom corner, match side seam to bottom fold and sew across corner 2" from point (Fig. 1).

Fig. 1

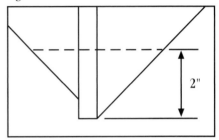

2. Turn bag right side out.
3. Trace patterns, this page, onto tracing paper. Use patterns to cut four leaves from green felt, one stem from black felt, one acorn from brown felt, and one acorn cap from dark brown felt.
4. Overlapping shapes as necessary, glue two leaves, stem, acorn, and acorn cap to front of bag. Work *Blanket Stitches* to outline stem, acorn, and acorn cap and *Running Stitches* to add veins to leaves.
5. Place gift in bag. Tie felt strip into a bow around top of bag.
6. For tag, draw around leaf pattern on card stock; cut out ¹/₈" inside drawn lines. Use marker to draw "stitches" along edges and to write message on tag. Glue tag to one felt leaf. Use three strands of green floss to attach remaining leaves to bow.

DAZZLING PARTY FAVORS

*L*ittle girls will love these pretty party favors! The Punchy Fudge has a delightful fruit flavor that will bring raves from everyone. Add pairs of glamorous earrings to the boxes for dazzle.

PUNCHY FUDGE

- 3 cups sugar
- ³/₄ cup butter or margarine
- 1 can (5 ounces) evaporated milk
- 1 package (12 ounces) white baking chips
- 1 jar (7 ounces) marshmallow creme
- 1 teaspoon vanilla extract
- ³/₄ teaspoon unsweetened punch-flavored soft drink mix

Line a 9-inch square baking pan with foil, extending foil over 2 sides of pan; grease foil. Butter sides of a heavy large saucepan. Combine sugar, butter, and evaporated milk in saucepan. Attach a candy thermometer to pan, making sure thermometer does not touch bottom of pan. Stirring constantly, bring to a boil over medium heat. Boil 5 minutes or until thermometer reaches 234 degrees. Remove from heat. Gradually stir in baking chips until melted. Add marshmallow creme, vanilla, and drink mix; stir until well blended. Spread mixture into prepared pan. Cool completely.

Use ends of foil to lift fudge from pan. Cut into 1-inch squares. Store in an airtight container in a cool place.

Yield: about 5¹/₂ dozen pieces fudge

FANCY PARTY FAVORS

For each flavor, you will need an oval papier-mâché Shaker box (we used a 3⁵/₈" x 4⁵/₈" box), pink card stock, ¹/₄" dia. hole punch, 17" of ⁵/₈"w white sheer ribbon, hot glue gun, two 15mm white and two 7mm pink acrylic jewels, two 3" white craft feathers, two earring clips, two coordinating pieces of wrapping paper, spray adhesive, ³/₄"w white flat lace trim, 1"w white grosgrain ribbon, and craft glue.

1. Draw around box lid on card stock; cut out ³/₄" inside drawn line. Working at one narrow end of oval, punch one hole close to edge and two holes ¹/₂" apart 1" from edge. Thread ribbon through hole close to edge and tie ends into a bow at front.
2. For each earring, glue one white and one pink jewel to base of quill of one feather. Glue clip to back of white jewel.
3. Insert earring clips through remaining holes in card stock; close clips.

4. Draw around lid on wrong side of one wrapping paper piece. Cut out paper piece ¹/₂" outside drawn line. Clip edge at ¹/₂" intervals to ¹/₄" from drawn line. Apply spray adhesive to wrong side of paper. Smooth paper onto top and side of lid.
5. Measure around box lid; add ¹/₂". Cut one piece each from ribbon and trim the determined measurement. Overlapping ends, use craft glue to glue trim, then ribbon around lid. Glue back of bow to top of lid.
6. Measure height of box; add ³/₄". Measure around box; add ¹/₂". Cut a piece from remaining wrapping paper the determined measurements. Apply spray adhesive to wrong side of paper. With paper extending at top and bottom of box and overlapping short edges, smooth paper onto side of box. Glue top edge to inside of box and bottom edge to bottom of box.

FIT FOR A PRINCESS

*F*it for a princess, our delicious White Chocolate Chewies are a regal gift idea for any young lady. A frilly craft foam charm hung from shimmery braid makes a cute necklace for her to enjoy when the chocolates are gone.

WHITE CHOCOLATE CHEWIES

1	package (14 ounces) caramels
1/4	cup evaporated milk
1	cup chopped pecans, toasted
1	cup crispy rice cereal
10	ounces vanilla candy coating, chopped
4	ounces white baking chocolate, chopped

Combine caramels and evaporated milk in top of a double boiler over simmering water; stir until smooth. Turn off heat; leave caramel mixture over warm water. Stir in pecans and cereal. Drop mixture by teaspoonfuls onto a heavily greased baking sheet. Chill 1 hour.

Melt candy coating and white chocolate in top of double boiler over hot, not simmering, water. Remove from heat. Dip candies into chocolate mixture. Return to baking sheet. Chill candies 30 minutes or until chocolate hardens. Store in an airtight container in a cool place.

Yield: about 4 dozen candies

FRILLY SWEETHEART NECKLACE

For necklace, you will need tracing paper; pink craft foam; decorative-edge craft scissors; white, red, and green

dimensional paint; hole punch; and 26" of silver braided cord.

For gift box, you will *also* need a gift box with white lid (we used a 4 1/2" x 7 1/4" x 1 1/4"d box) and ribbons to tie around box (we used 30" each of 2"w white sheer ribbon with silver edge, 7/8"w pink satin ribbon, and 15" of 1/8"w white satin ribbon).

Follow Painting Techniques, page 122, for painting tips.

1. Trace pattern, page 117, onto tracing paper; cut out. Draw around heart on craft foam. Use craft scissors to cut out heart along drawn line.

2. Use paint to freehand designs on heart (we painted dots, lines, and flowers).

3. Punch hole in center top of heart. Fold cord in half; thread folded end through hole. Thread ends of cord through loop and pull gently; knot ends together.

4. Place gift in box; replace lid. Folding cord to fit on bow and catching folded cord in knot, tie ribbons into a bow around box.

MUCHAS GRACIAS!

*S*ay Muchas Gracias *with a jar of tangy Margarita Jelly! You'll want to include some cream cheese and crispy pretzel chips for munching. An easy-to-fuse table scarf accompanies the gift for a lasting surprise, and the cute cactus tag is fun to make from craft foam.*

MARGARITA JELLY

1¹/₂ cups freshly squeezed lime juice
¹/₂ cup freshly squeezed orange juice
1 cup water
1 package (1³/₄ ounces) powdered fruit pectin
4¹/₂ cups sugar
¹/₄ cup tequila
1 teaspoon grated lime zest
2 drops green liquid food coloring
Lime peel strips
Cream cheese and pretzel crackers to give

In a large Dutch oven, combine fruit juices, water, and pectin over medium-high heat. Bring to a rolling boil. Add sugar. Stirring constantly, bring to a rolling boil again and boil 1 minute. Remove from heat; skim off foam. Stir in tequila, lime zest, and food coloring. Place a lime strip in each heat-resistant jar. Spoon jelly into jars; cover and cool to room temperature. Store in refrigerator. Give with cream cheese and crackers.

Yield: about 6¹/₂ cups jelly

"MUCHAS GRACIAS!" TABLE SCARF AND GIFT TAG

For table scarf, you will need ⁵/₈"w paper-backed fusible web tape, 11³/₄" x 47¹/₄" piece of fabric, fabric glue, and two 10¹/₂" lengths of 2"w fringe.

For gift tag, you will *also* need tracing paper; light orange, red, green, and brown craft foam; craft glue; black permanent medium-point and fine-point markers; decorative-edge craft scissors; toothpick; and orange acrylic paint.

Allow glue to dry after each application.

1. For table scarf, follow manufacturer's instructions to fuse web tape along long edges on wrong side of fabric. Do not remove paper backing. Press each edge ⁵/₈" to wrong side. Unfold edges and remove paper backing. Refold edge and fuse in place. Repeat to hem short edges. Center and glue fringe along each short edge on wrong side of scarf.

2. For gift tag, trace patterns, page 119, onto tracing paper; cut out. Use patterns to cut cactus and limb from green foam and sign from brown foam.

3. Use craft glue to glue sign to orange foam and cactus and limb to red foam. Leaving a ¹/₁₆" orange border, cut out sign. Use medium-point marker to write message on sign. Leaving a ¹/₈" red border, use craft scissors to cut out cactus and limb. Glue limb and sign to cactus.

4. Use fine-point marker to make "X's" on cactus and limb. Use end of toothpick to paint orange dots on cactus tips.

TROPICAL MINI CAKES

*P*erfect for group gifts, *these nutty mini cakes are packed with big tropical taste. Deliver each cake in a lined aluminum pan accented with a spray of ribbon and faux fruit.*

TROPICAL FRUIT-NUT CAKES

- 1 cup butter or margarine, softened
- 2 cups sugar
- 6 eggs
- ⅔ cup milk
- 2 packages (4 ounces each) candied pineapple, chopped
- 1 package (7 ounces) flaked coconut
- 1 cup chopped pecans
- 2 packages (11 ounces each) vanilla wafers, crushed

Preheat oven to 325 degrees. In a large bowl, cream butter and sugar until fluffy. Add eggs and milk; beat until smooth. Stir in pineapple, coconut, and pecans. Stir in vanilla wafer crumbs. Spoon mixture into a well-greased 6-mold fluted tube pan, filling each mold about three-fourths full. Bake about 34 to 38 minutes or until a toothpick inserted in center of cake comes out clean. Cool in pan 5 minutes. Remove from pan and cool completely on a wire rack. Repeat with remaining batter. Store in an airtight container.

Yield: about 12 mini cakes

FRUITY SERVING PAN

You will need a drawing compass, tissue paper, decorative-edge craft scissors, 6" dia. aluminum frying pan, 1½"w ribbon, and an artificial fruit pick.

1. Use compass to draw a 6" circle on tissue paper. Use craft scissors to cut out circle along drawn line; place in pan.

2. Tie ribbon into a bow around handle of pan; insert pick under bow.

DON'T GO BANANAS!

To keep your friends from "going bananas" during the holidays, entice them to relax with yummy Banana Fruitcakes! These power-packed treats make great offerings when tucked in paper gift bags trimmed with ribbon and decorative fruit.

BANANA FRUITCAKES

1 package (18¼ ounces) butter-recipe yellow cake mix with pudding in the mix
1¼ cups mashed bananas (about 3 bananas)
3 eggs
½ cup cream of coconut
¼ cup vegetable oil
1½ cups flaked coconut
1½ cups chopped pecans
1 cup chopped dates
1 package (4 ounces) red candied cherries, chopped
1 package (4 ounces) green candied cherries, chopped

Preheat oven to 325 degrees. Grease five 3¼ x 6-inch loaf pans. Line pans with waxed paper; grease paper. In a large bowl, combine cake mix, bananas, eggs, cream of coconut, and oil; beat until well blended. Stir in coconut, pecans, dates, and cherries. Spoon batter into prepared pans. Bake 50 to 55 minutes or until a toothpick inserted in center of cake comes out clean. Cool in pans 10 minutes. Remove from pans. Cool completely on a wire rack. Store in an airtight container.

Yield: 5 fruitcakes

"GO BANANAS!" BAG

You will need a gift bag with removable handles (we used a 6⅛" x 10½" bag), ⅜"w grosgrain ribbon, ⅜"w plaid ribbon, hot glue gun, artificial greenery (we used pine and holly berry stems), and three 2½" artificial bananas.
For gift tag, you will *also* need 2" x 4" piece of white poster board and a black permanent fine-point marker.

1. Remove handles from bag. Measure length of one handle. Cut two lengths of grosgrain ribbon the determined measurement. Thread ends through handle holes; knot ends inside bag.
2. Cut one 12" length each of grosgrain and plaid ribbons. Tie each ribbon into a bow. Glue greenery, bananas, and bows together on front of bag.
3. For tag, cut corners from one end of poster board to form a point. Use marker to write message on tag. Glue tag to front of bag.

CHRISTMAS CONFETTI

*F*lecked with yellow pepper, green olives, and pimiento, colorful Confetti Spread is a festival of flavor! Top off a tree-shaped serving dish with a well-wishing star to "spread" Yuletide cheer.

CONFETTI SPREAD

- 2 packages (8 ounces each) cream cheese, softened
- 2 teaspoons caraway seed
- 2 teaspoons dried basil leaves
- 2 teaspoons dried dill weed
- 2 teaspoons dried chives
- 1/2 teaspoon garlic salt
- 1/2 teaspoon lemon pepper
- 3 tablespoons chopped yellow pepper
- 3 tablespoons chopped stuffed green olives
- 3 tablespoons finely chopped pecans, toasted
- 3 tablespoons diced pimiento
- 3 tablespoons chopped fresh parsley
- 3 tablespoons chopped red onion
- 3 tablespoons chopped black olives
- 3 tablespoons sunflower kernels
  Crackers to serve

In a large bowl, combine cream cheese, caraway seed, basil, dill weed, chives, garlic salt, and lemon pepper; beat until well blended. Stir in remaining ingredients. Spread cheese mixture into a 3-cup dish (we used a 9-inch-high plastic tree-shaped dish). Cover and store in refrigerator. Serve with crackers.

Yield: about 3 cups spread

CHRISTMAS STAR TAG

You will need photocopy of tag design (page 118) on card stock, colored pencils, and double-sided tape.

1. Use pencils to color tag; cut out.
2. Use tape to secure tag to gift.

CAKE TO GO

Mocha-
Chocolate Chip
Cake Mix

Mocha
Icing Mix

Happiness is lickin' the spoon!

*B*usy cooks are sure to appreciate this handy cake kit! All the dry ingredients needed for the cake and icing are packaged in fabric bags and presented with baking instructions. A country basket lined with shredded paper and a wooden spoon complete the homey gift.

MOCHA-CHOCOLATE CHIP CAKE MIX

CAKE MIX
1 package (18$\frac{1}{4}$ ounces) devil's food cake mix with pudding in the mix
1 cup semisweet chocolate mini chips
1$\frac{1}{2}$ tablespoons instant coffee granules

ICING MIX
2 cups chocolate-flavored confectioners sugar
1 teaspoon instant coffee granules

For cake mix, combine cake mix, chocolate chips, and coffee granules. Store in an airtight container.

For icing mix, sift confectioners sugar and coffee granules into a small bowl. Store in an airtight container.

Give mixes with baking instructions.

Yield: 1 cake mix and 1 icing mix

To bake: Preheat oven to 350 degrees. In a large bowl, combine cake mix, 1$\frac{1}{3}$ cups water, 3 eggs, and $\frac{1}{4}$ cup vegetable oil; beat until well blended. Pour batter into a greased 9 x 13-inch baking pan. Bake 30 to 34 minutes or until a toothpick inserted in center of cake comes out clean. Cool cake in pan.

Combine icing mix and $\frac{1}{4}$ cup boiling water in a small bowl; stir until smooth. Pour icing over cake. Let cake cool. Store cake in an airtight container.

Yield: 12 to 15 servings

"LICKIN' THE SPOON" BASKET

BAGS
For each bag, you will need an 8" x 20$\frac{1}{4}$" piece of fabric for bag, $\frac{5}{8}$"w fusible web tape, one 2" x 4$\frac{1}{2}$" piece each of paper-backed fusible web and light-colored fabric for label, one 3" x 5$\frac{1}{2}$" piece each of paper-backed fusible web and fabric for label border, brown permanent medium-point marker, a large-eye needle, gold pearl cotton, and a 1" dia. wooden button.

1. Matching right sides and short edges, press fabric piece for bag in half. Unfold fabric and follow manufacturer's instructions to fuse web tape along each long edge on right side. Refold fabric and fuse edges together. Fuse web tape along top edge on wrong side of bag; do not remove paper backing. Fold top of bag $\frac{5}{8}$" to wrong side; press. Unfold and remove paper backing. Refold and fuse in place. Turn bag right side out.

2. For label, fuse web pieces to wrong side of fabrics for label and label border; do not remove paper backing from border fabric. Center and fuse label to label border. Use marker to write name of mix on label. Remove paper backing and fuse label to front of bag. Place gift in corresponding bag.

3. Fold top of bag 1" to front. Thread pearl cotton through fold and holes in button; tie into a bow at front of bag.

TAG
You will need craft glue, 2$\frac{1}{2}$" x 3" piece of light-colored card stock for tag, 3$\frac{1}{4}$" x 3$\frac{3}{4}$" piece of card stock for border, brown permanent medium-point marker, hole punch, 20" of jute twine, and a wooden mixing spoon.

Center and glue light-colored card stock to card stock for border. Use marker to write message on tag and to draw an "X" in each corner and "stitches" along edges of border. Punch hole in tag; use twine to tie tag to spoon.

BASKET
You will need a basket (we used a 10$\frac{1}{2}$"w x 6"h heart-shaped basket) and shredded paper.

Arrange shredded paper, bags, and tag in basket.

SANTA'S CHERRY POPCORN

*C*herry Popcorn is a colorful sensation! Our ho-ho-homemade recipe makes a lot, so you'll have plenty for all the snack-lovers on the jolly gentleman's list. Package the bright-colored snack in a bag sporting a Santa cutout to show off your festive offerings.

CHERRY POPCORN

	Vegetable cooking spray
16	cups popped popcorn
2	cups sugar
1/2	cup light corn syrup
2	teaspoons cherry flavoring
1	teaspoon salt
1	teaspoon baking soda
	Red paste food coloring

Spray inside of a 14 x 20-inch oven cooking bag with cooking spray. Place popcorn in bag. In a 2-quart microwave-safe bowl, combine sugar and corn syrup. Microwave on high power (100%) until mixture boils, about 2 minutes. Stir and microwave 2 minutes longer. Stir in cherry flavoring, salt, and baking soda; tint red. Pour syrup over popcorn; stir and shake until well coated. Microwave on high power 3 minutes, stirring and shaking after each minute (mixture will be hot). Spread on aluminum foil sprayed with cooking spray to cool. Store in an airtight container.

Yield: about 17 cups candied popcorn

SANTA CUTOUT BAG

You will need tracing paper; transfer paper; small white paper bag (we used a 4³/₄" x 9" bag); peach, red, and black colored pencils; black permanent fine-point marker; small sharp scissors; decorative-edge craft scissors; 30" square of red cellophane; and 1 yd. of ⁵/₈"w green satin ribbon.

1. Trace pattern, page 119, onto tracing paper. Use transfer paper to transfer Santa to front of bag.
2. Use colored pencils to color mittens and boots black; hat and body red; and face peach.

3. Use marker to outline hat brim, pom-pom, face, beard, mittens, and boots with a solid line; hat and body with a dashed line; and make dots for eyes. Draw scattered snowflakes on bag.
4. Cutting close to outlines, use small sharp scissors to carefully cut out body and hat.
5. Use craft scissors to trim top of bag.
6. Place cellophane then gift in bag. Gather cellophane over gift and tie ribbon into a bow around gathers.

CRANBERRY STOCKING STUFFERS

*F*or a sweet stocking stuffer, try Cranberry Christmas Cookies. The popular holiday berries add tart flavor to our mouth-watering goodies. Drop them in easy-to-make dish towel stockings for quick and inexpensive Yuletide gifts.

CRANBERRY CHRISTMAS COOKIES

1 cup fresh cranberries
1/2 cup vegetable shortening
1 1/2 cups sugar
1 egg
2 tablespoons buttermilk
1 teaspoon vanilla extract
1/4 teaspoon orange extract
2 cups all-purpose flour
1/2 teaspoon baking soda
1/2 teaspoon ground cinnamon
1/2 teaspoon ground cloves
1/2 teaspoon ground nutmeg
1/4 teaspoon salt
1 cup chopped walnuts
1 cup golden raisins

Preheat oven to 375 degrees. Process cranberries in a food processor until coarsely ground. In a large bowl, cream shortening and sugar until fluffy. Add egg, buttermilk, and extracts; beat until smooth. Stir in cranberries. In a small bowl, combine flour, baking soda, cinnamon, cloves, nutmeg, and salt. Add dry ingredients to creamed mixture; stir until a soft dough forms. Stir in walnuts and raisins. Drop teaspoonfuls of dough onto a greased baking sheet. Bake 9 to 11 minutes or until bottoms are lightly browned. Transfer cookies to a wire rack to cool. Store in an airtight container.

Yield: about 7 dozen cookies

DISH TOWEL STOCKINGS

For each stocking, you will need tracing paper, dish towel (at least 24" long), 12" of 7/8"w wired ribbon, 1" dia. button, embroidery floss, and a purchased gift tag with hanger.

1. Matching dashed lines and arrows, trace stocking top and stocking bottom patterns, page 120, onto tracing paper; cut out.
2. Matching right sides and short edges, fold towel in half. Align top of pattern with hemmed edge of towel; draw around pattern. Leaving top edge open, follow Steps 2 and 3 of *Sewing Shapes*, page 123, to make stocking.
3. For hanger, fold ribbon in half to form a loop. Use floss to sew button and loop to stocking front at heel seam. Trim top ribbon end. Write message on tag. Hang tag on button.

GINGERBREAD BEAR HUGS

*D*eliver a bagful of bear hugs to a teddy-loving friend. Our Quick Gingerbread Cookies are deliciously easy to make — simply knead a few extra ingredients into a roll of ready-to-bake dough. For a huggable presentation, cover a paper bag with fun print fabric and top it with a cute bear crafted from wooden cutouts.

QUICK GINGERBREAD COOKIES

- 1 package (1 pound, 2 ounces) refrigerated sugar cookie dough
- 2 teaspoons molasses
- 1/4 to 1/2 cup all-purpose flour, divided
- 1 tablespoon ground cinnamon
- 1/8 teaspoon ground ginger
- 1 to 2 teaspoons cocoa (optional)

Preheat oven to 350 degrees. Flatten dough on a lightly floured surface. Drizzle molasses over dough. Sprinkle 1/4 cup flour, cinnamon, and ginger over dough. For a darker dough, add cocoa with dry ingredients. Knead ingredients into dough until well blended, using additional flour as necessary. On a lightly floured surface, use a floured rolling pin to roll out dough to 1/4-inch thickness. Use a cookie cutter to cut out dough (we used a 3 1/2 x 4-inch bear-shaped cutter). Transfer to a greased baking sheet. Bake 6 to 8 minutes or until bottoms are lightly browned. Transfer cookies to a wire rack to cool. Store in an airtight container.

Yield: about 1 dozen cookies

TEDDY BEAR PARTY PACK

You will need tracing paper, transfer paper, 2 1/4"h wooden heart cutout for head, three 2" long wooden teardrop cutouts for legs and muzzle, craft knife, cutting mat, utility scissors, tan and brown acrylic paint, paintbrushes, hot glue gun, black permanent fine-point marker, spring-type clothespin, 18" of 5/8"w satin ribbon, lunch-size paper bag, fabric, spray adhesive, and decorative-edge craft scissors.

Use hot glue for all gluing unless otherwise indicated. Allow paint and glue to dry after each application.

1. Trace bear patterns, page 120, onto tracing paper. Use transfer paper to transfer outside lines of head to heart and muzzle to one teardrop.
2. Use craft knife to score along transferred lines; cut out shapes with utility scissors. Glue points of remaining teardrop shapes to back of head for legs.
3. Paint muzzle and inner ears tan. Paint remaining portion of head and legs brown.
4. Use transfer paper to transfer details to head and muzzle. Use marker to draw over all transferred lines, add outlines to head and legs, and draw claws on paws. Glue muzzle to head. Glue bear to clothespin. Tie ribbon into a bow; glue to clothespin below bear's head.
5. Draw around front of bag on fabric. Cut out 1/4" inside drawn lines. Apply spray adhesive to wrong side of fabric; smooth over front of bag. Use craft scissors to trim top of bag.
6. Place gift in bag. Fold top of bag 1 1/2" to front. Clip bear on bag.

CHRISTMAS CRUNCHIES

*M*ake a bundle of these no-bake nuggets to delight co-workers or classmates. Simply stir crunchy ingredients like cinnamon graham cereal and pretzels together with a creamy butterscotch coating. You'll have plenty of melt-in-your-mouth morsels to share!

BUTTERSCOTCH CRUNCHIES

These candies set up quickly; ask a friend to help drop candies.

 1 package (15¼ ounces) cinnamon graham cereal
1½ cups dry-roasted peanuts
2½ cups broken small pretzel sticks
 ½ cup butter or margarine
 14 ounces vanilla candy coating, chopped
 4 cups miniature marshmallows
 ¼ cup whipping cream
 1 cup butterscotch chips

Combine cereal, peanuts, and pretzels in a very large bowl. In a heavy large saucepan, melt butter over low heat. Add candy coating, marshmallows, and whipping cream. Stirring frequently, cook over low heat until mixture is smooth and marshmallows are almost melted. Remove from heat; add butterscotch chips. Stir until chips melt and mixture is smooth. Pour over cereal mixture; stir until well coated. Quickly drop by tablespoonfuls onto greased waxed paper. Let stand 2 hours or until candy hardens. Store in an airtight container in a cool place.

Yield: about 12 dozen candies

SNOWBALL DELIGHTS

*Y*ou can stir up several gifts in no time with easy-to-make Orange-Nut Snowballs! The frosty cookies are yummy gifts for neighbors, Sunday school classmates, or other groups. For each gift, fill a decorative tin and wrap it in cellophane with a colorful bow and tag — what could be easier!

ORANGE-NUT SNOWBALLS

  1 cup butter or margarine, softened
  2 cups confectioners sugar, divided
  1 teaspoon grated orange zest
  1 teaspoon orange extract
$1/2$ teaspoon vanilla extract
$2^{1}/4$ cups all-purpose flour
$1/4$ teaspoon salt
  1 cup chopped walnuts, toasted and coarsely ground

Preheat oven to 350 degrees. In a large bowl, cream butter and $1/2$ cup confectioners sugar until fluffy. Stir in orange zest and extracts. In a medium bowl, combine flour and salt. Add dry ingredients to creamed mixture; stir until a soft dough forms. Stir in walnuts. Shape dough into 1-inch balls and place 2 inches apart on an ungreased baking sheet. Bake 12 to 15 minutes or until bottoms are lightly browned. Roll warm cookies in remaining $1^{1}/2$ cups confectioners sugar. Place cookies on waxed paper; cool completely. Roll in confectioners sugar again. Store in an airtight container.

Yield: about 4 dozen cookies

SNOWY DAY GIFT PACKAGE

You will need 32" of 3"w wired ribbon, 12" of floral wire, snowflake ornament with hanger, cellophane, and a decorative container (we used a 5" x 7" oval silver metallic container with snowflake cutouts).

For tag, you will *also* need decorative-edge craft scissors, construction paper, 1" x 1³/8" Christmas-motif sticker, black permanent fine-point and medium-point markers, and double-sided tape.

1. Follow *Making a Bow,* page 121, to make a bow with two 6" loops, one 3" center loop, and two 6" streamers. Thread ornament onto wire of bow.

2. Place gift in container; place container at center of cellophane. Gather cellophane around container. Wrap wire ends of bow around gathers; twist wire to secure.

3. For tag, use craft scissors to cut a 2" x 3" piece from construction paper. Apply sticker to tag. Use fine-point marker to draw "stitches" along edges and medium-point marker to write message on tag. Use tape to attach tag to bow.

SIMPLY SAUCY

*P*our our Chocolate-
Peanut Butter Sauce over
ice cream or cake and watch
the desserts disappear! The
microwavable sauce can be
served warm, so it makes a
great addition to winter treats.
Pack a jar of the sweet stuff
in a snowman gift can for a
simple winter offering.

CHOCOLATE-PEANUT BUTTER SAUCE

    1   cup firmly packed brown sugar
    1   cup whipping cream
  ¹/₂ cup crunchy peanut butter
    1   cup milk chocolate chips
    1   teaspoon vanilla extract

Whisk brown sugar and whipping
cream in a medium microwave-safe bowl
until smooth. Whisk in peanut butter and
microwave on high power (100%)
2 minutes. Whisk in chocolate chips and
vanilla until smooth. Serve warm or at
room temperature over ice cream or
cake. Store in an airtight container in
refrigerator.

Yield: about 2³/₄ cups sauce

SNOWMAN GIFT CAN

You will need a 3¹/₄" dia. x 3¹/₂"h can,
spray primer, white and blue spray paint,
hammer, nail, 14" of 20-gauge white
cloth-covered wire, tracing paper, white
craft foam, orange and black permanent
fine-point markers, ¹/₂" x 6" torn fabric
strip, and a low temperature glue gun.
For jar lid cover, you will *also* need a
5¹/₂" square of fabric, pint jar with lid,
rubber band, and 16" of ¹/₈"w ribbon.

*Allow primer and paint to dry after
each application.*

1. Spray can with primer, then blue paint.
Lightly spray can with white paint.
2. For handle, use hammer and nail to
make a hole on each side of can. Insert
wire end into one hole; bend up to
secure. Repeat for opposite side.
3. Trace pattern, page 118, onto tracing
paper; cut out. Use pattern to cut

snowman from craft foam. Use markers to
draw face and buttons on snowman.
4. For scarf, fray short edges of fabric
strip. Glue scarf around snowman's neck.
Glue snowman to can.
5. For jar lid cover, fray all edges of fabric
square. Place fabric over lid; secure with
rubber band. Tie ribbon into a bow over
rubber band.

*I*t's easy to chase away the chill of winter when you share Pineapple Cider Mix with a friend. Just add hot water for a fruity warmer! For added cheer, offer the mixture in a pineapple look-alike — a bag dressed up using colored paper twist and markers.

PINEAPPLE CIDER MIX

- 1 package (7.4 ounces) apple cider mix (10 envelopes)
- 1 package (3 ounces) pineapple gelatin
- 2 packages (0.15 ounce each) unsweetened orange-pineapple-flavored soft drink mix
- 2 cups sugar

In a medium bowl, combine apple cider mix, gelatin, soft drink mix, and sugar. Store in an airtight container. Give with serving instructions.

Yield: about 3 1/4 cups mix

To serve: Pour 6 ounces hot water over 2 tablespoons cider mix; stir until well blended.

PAPER TWIST PINEAPPLE BAG

You will need brown paper gift bag with handles (we used a 5 1/4" x 8 1/4" bag); yellow and green paper twist (5 3/4"w untwisted); orange, red-orange, and brown medium-point permanent markers; ruler; and a hot glue gun.

For gift tag, you will *also* need tracing paper, brown kraft paper, green permanent medium-point marker, drawing compass, yellow card stock, decorative-edge craft scissors, hole punch, and 12" of 1/8"w green ribbon.

1. Measure height of bag; add 1 1/2". Cut two pieces of yellow paper twist the determined measurement.
2. For pineapple design, use red-orange marker and ruler to draw a 3/4" diamond grid on one side of each piece of paper twist. Use brown marker to add a dot at center of each diamond. Use orange marker to draw a "V" at bottom of each diamond.
3. For leaf sections, cut two 6" lengths of green paper twist. Spacing evenly, make three 5" cuts in each length. Twist ends of each leaf (Fig. 1).

Fig. 1

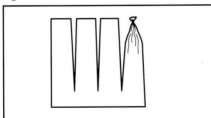

4. Gathering bottom edge of one leaf section to 3"w, glue to front of bag at top. Repeat for back of bag.
5. Fold top of one pineapple design 3/4" to wrong side; gather fold to 3"w. Matching fold to bottom of leaf section, glue pineapple over front of bag; glue excess to bottom of bag. Repeat for back of bag.
6. Trace tag pattern, this page, onto tracing paper. Use pattern to cut tag from kraft paper. Use green marker to write message on tag.
7. For pineapple slice, use compass to draw a 3" dia. circle on card stock. Using craft scissors, cut along drawn line. Use red-orange marker to outline edge and orange marker to add details to slice.
8. Punch one hole each in tag and slice. Punch two holes at top of bag close to each side of pineapple. Place gift in bag. Thread ribbon ends through holes in bag, slice, and tag; knot ends together.

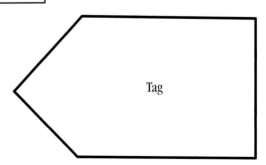

Tag

PATTERNS

Cloud

CASSEROLE PAN TOPPER
(page 7)

Tree

Sun

Roof

ST. PADDY'S PRETZEL JAR
(page 14)

CUPID JAR TOPPER
(page 10)

"HOMEMADE PICKLES" JAR

(page 15)

Leisure Arts, Inc., grants permission to the owner of this book to photocopy the "Homemade Pickles" jar label design on this page for personal use only.

FLOWER-STAMPED CANDY DISH

(page 17)

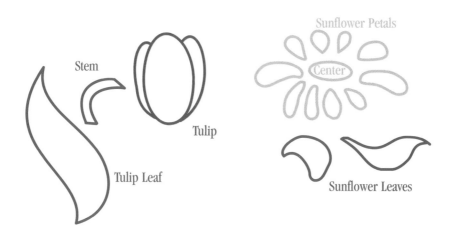

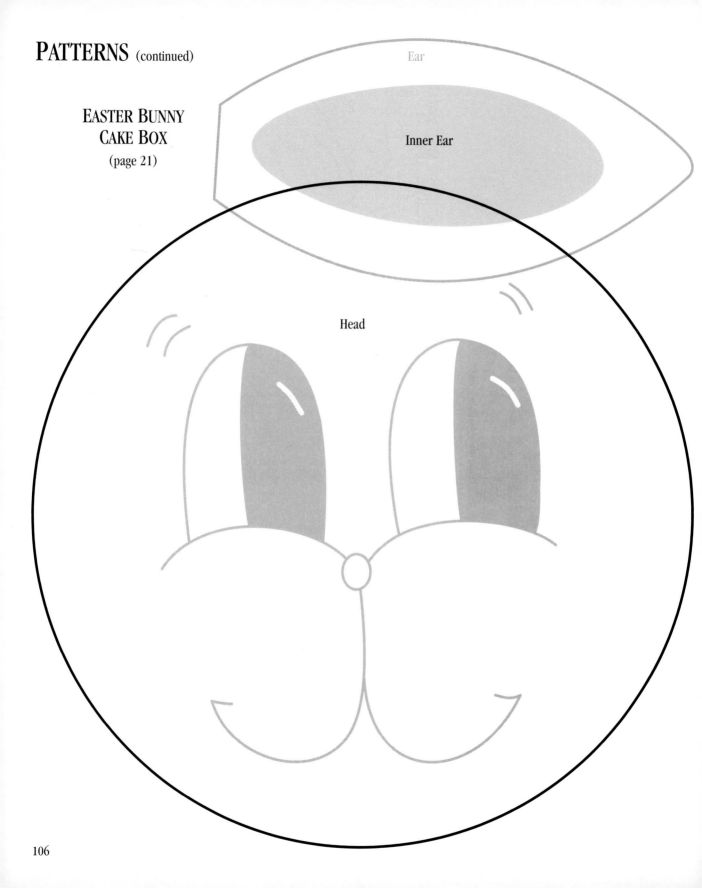

PATTERNS (continued)

EASTER BUNNY
CAKE BOX
(page 21)

Ear

Inner Ear

Head

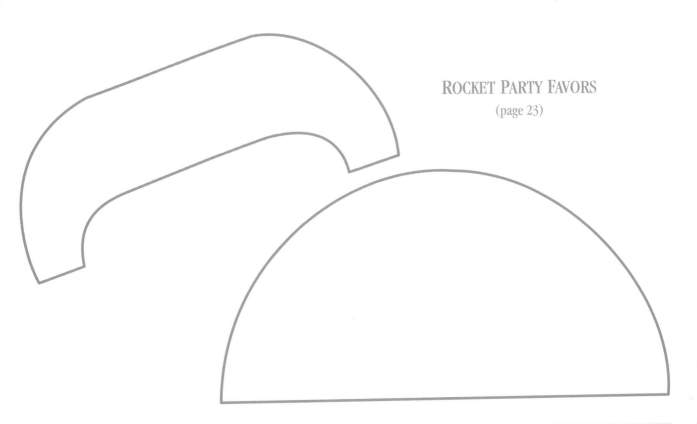

ROCKET PARTY FAVORS
(page 23)

GIFT BAG AND MUG
(page 26)

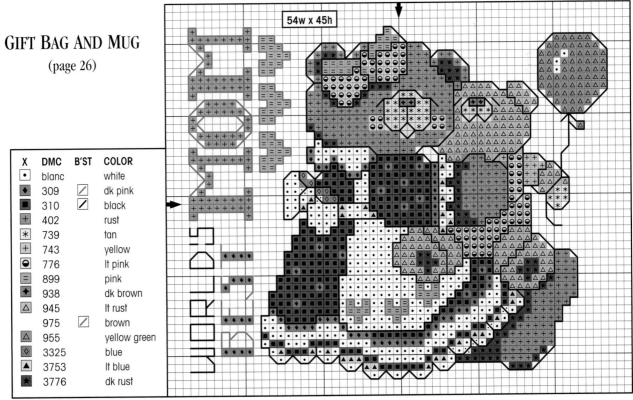

54w x 45h

X	DMC	B'ST	COLOR
•	blanc		white
◆	309	⟋	dk pink
■	310	⟋	black
+	402		rust
*	739		tan
+	743		yellow
◓	776		lt pink
=	899		pink
✦	938		dk brown
△	945		lt rust
	975	⟋	brown
△	955		yellow green
◇	3325		blue
▲	3753		lt blue
★	3776		dk rust

107

PATTERNS (continued)

"TEACHERS RULE" GIFT BAGS
(page 30)

ALLIGATOR GIFT TOPPER
(page 31)

HONEY BEE GIFT ENSEMBLE
(page 35)

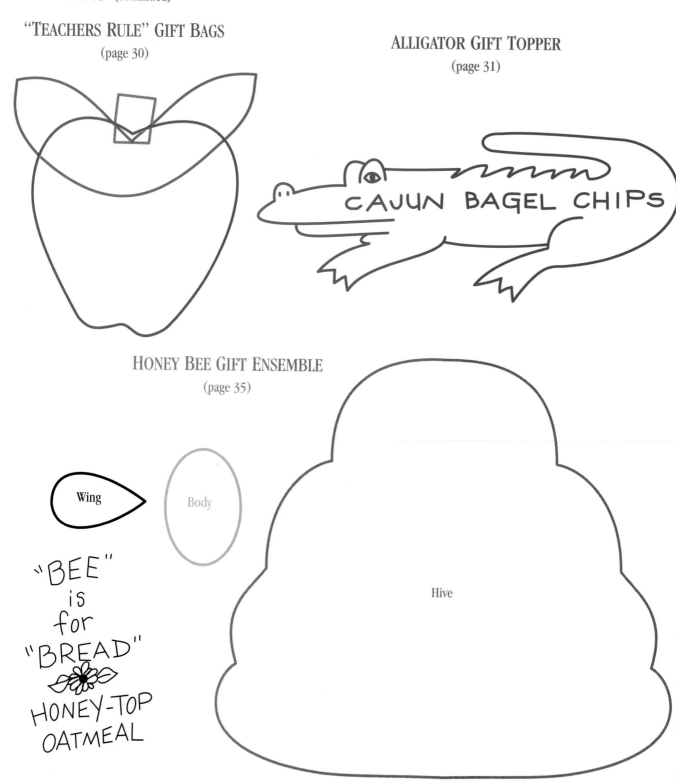

CAJUN BAGEL CHIPS

Wing

Body

Hive

"BEE"
is
for
"BREAD"
HONEY-TOP
OATMEAL

STRAWBERRY GIFT COLLECTION

(page 36)

Jar Lid

X	DMC	B'ST	COLOR
·	blanc		white
	310	∕	black
★	321		dk red
■	471		lt green
◉	498		vy dk red
□	666		red
=	743		yellow
✳	891		lt red
◆	986		vy dk green
△	987		dk green
+	989		green

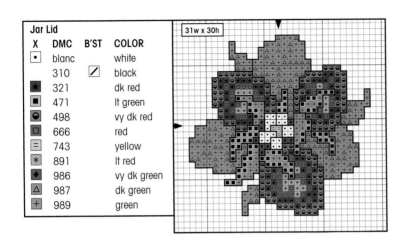

31w x 30h

RISE AND SHINE BASKET

(page 38)

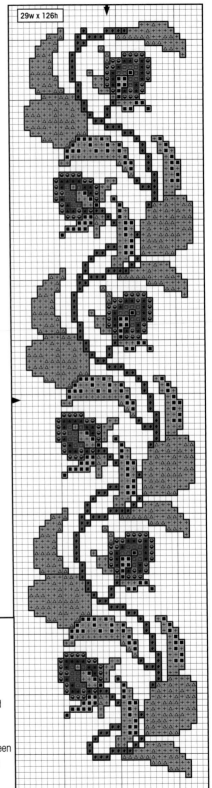

29w x 126h

Towel

X	DMC	B'ST	COLOR
	310	∕	black
★	321		dk red
■	471		lt green
◉	498		vy dk red
□	666		red
✳	891		lt red
◆	986		vy dk green
△	987		dk green
+	989		green

PATTERNS (continued)

"PICKLED" PRESENT
(page 46)

PICKLED GREEN BEANS

Leisure Arts, Inc., grants permission to the owner of this book to photocopy the "Pickled Green Beans" label design on this page for personal use only.

FABULOUS CATCH BASKET
(page 45)

Splash!

GENTLEMAN'S GIFT BOX
(page 56)

THANKS "BERRY" MUCH GIFT TAG
(page 43)

BERRY-ETCHED BOTTLE
(page 49)

"SALT OF THE EARTH" BASKET
(page 58)

BUCKET O' SPICY PECANS
(page 64)

TEACHER'S
BASKET
(page 65)

Hey, Cowpoke! Eat this with yer spurs on!

Leisure Arts, Inc., grants permission to the owner of this book to photocopy the cowboy boot tag design on this page for personal use only.

111

PATTERNS (continued)

COVERED BOOK BOX
(page 69)

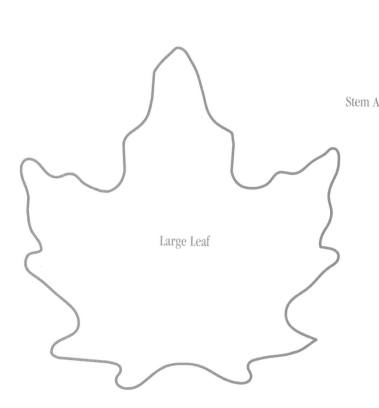

Sweet Indulgence by Fonda Chocolate

FALL SHAKER BOX
(page 71)

Small Leaf

Large Leaf

Stem A

Stem B

Stem C

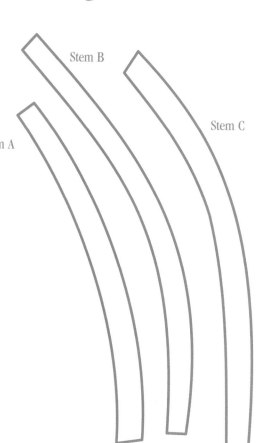

"HAPPY BIRTHDAY"
LOLLIPOP AND TAG
(page 67)

"CHEF'S SECRET" CANISTER
(page 73)

"WARM WELCOME" TAG
(page 75)

*Leisure Arts, Inc., grants permission to the owner
of this book to photocopy the "Welcome" tag
design on this page for personal use only.*

X	DMC	¼X	B'ST	COLOR
+	ecru	☐		ecru
★	300			vy dk rust
✳	301			rust
⊖	304	◢		rose
	309			lt rose
■	310		◢	black
▲	312	◢		dk blue
○	317			grey
★	322	◢		blue
△	400	◢		dk rust
✳	413			dk grey
⊙	420			gold
◓	435	◢		brown
✳	436			lt brown
+	471			lt green
◉	498	◢		red
☐	729	◢		lt gold
◇	739			lt tan
▲	815			dk red
■	3011			khaki green
◆	3346			dk green
✳	3347			green
=	3774	◢		peach
☆	3776	◢		lt rust
✦	3781			mocha brown
⊖	3799			charcoal grey
⊙	blanc			white Fr. Knot
⦿	310			black Fr. Knot

34w x 41h

35w x 37h

40w x 34h

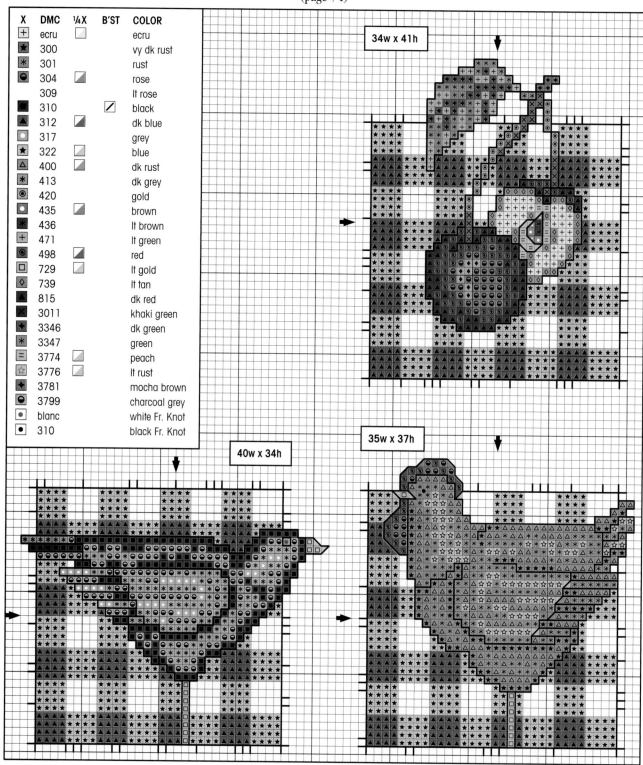

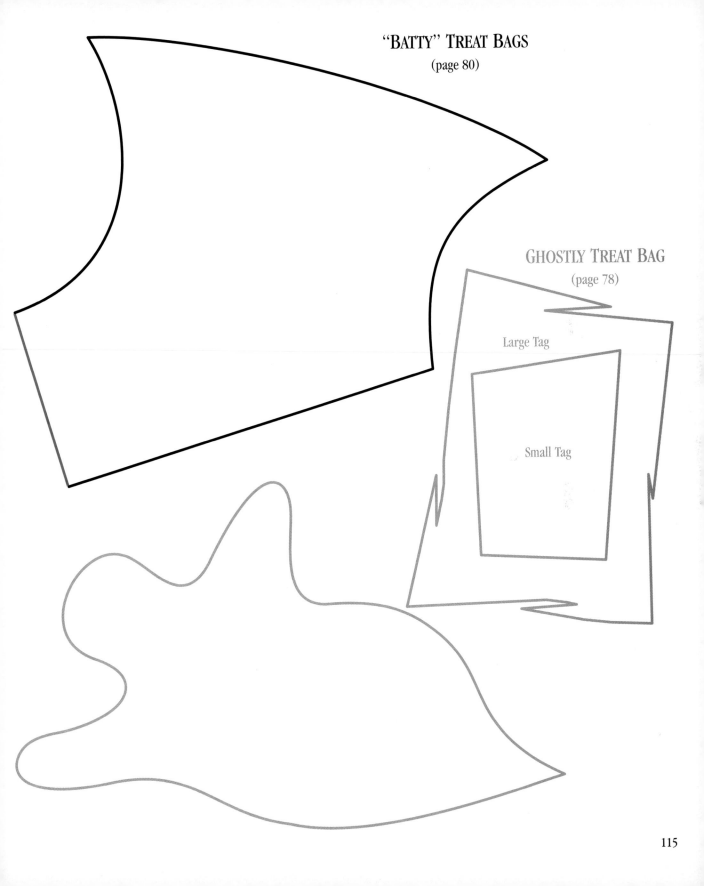

"Batty" Treat Bags
(page 80)

Ghostly Treat Bag
(page 78)

Large Tag

Small Tag

115

PATTERNS (continued)

GHOST COOKIES
(page 79)

MINI-TOTE
(page 79)

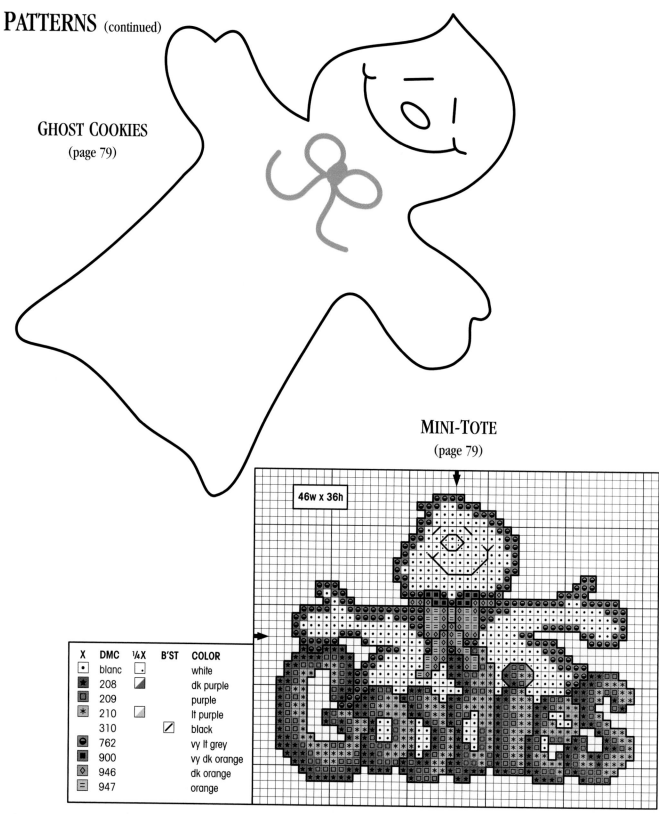

46w x 36h

X	DMC	¼X	B'ST	COLOR
•	blanc	•		white
★	208	◢		dk purple
▣	209			purple
✳	210	◢		lt purple
	310		◿	black
◉	762			vy lt grey
■	900			vy dk orange
◇	946			dk orange
=	947			orange

APPLE PIE "GOBBLER" BOX
(page 83)

FABRIC TUBES WITH
"COOKIE" TAGS
(page 85)

Turkey

Wing B

Wing A

FRILLY SWEETHEART NECKLACE
(page 89)

PATTERNS (continued)

COOKIE BASKET
(page 84)

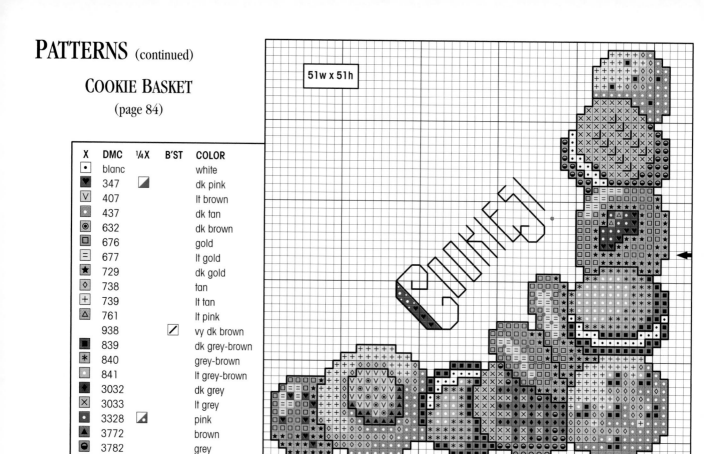

X	DMC	¼X	B'ST	COLOR
•	blanc			white
▼	347	◸		dk pink
V	407			lt brown
▫	437			dk tan
⊙	632			dk brown
▢	676			gold
≡	677			lt gold
★	729			dk gold
◇	738			tan
+	739			lt tan
△	761			lt pink
	938		◹	vy dk brown
▪	839			dk grey-brown
✳	840			grey-brown
▫	841			lt grey-brown
▪	3032			dk grey
✕	3033			lt grey
▫	3328	◿		pink
▲	3772			brown
◖	3782			grey
⊡	938	French Knot		vy dk brown

`51w x 51h`

CHRISTMAS STAR TAG
(page 93)

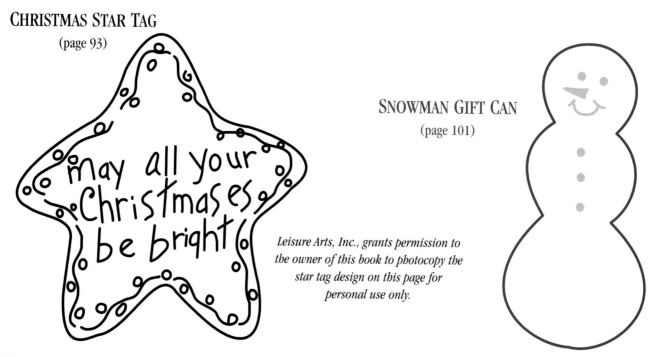

may all your Christmas es be bright

SNOWMAN GIFT CAN
(page 101)

Leisure Arts, Inc., grants permission to the owner of this book to photocopy the star tag design on this page for personal use only.

"MUCHAS GRACIAS!" TABLE
SCARF AND GIFT TAG

(page 90)

SANTA CUTOUT BAG

(page 96)

PATTERNS (continued)

TEDDY BEAR PARTY PACK
(page 98)

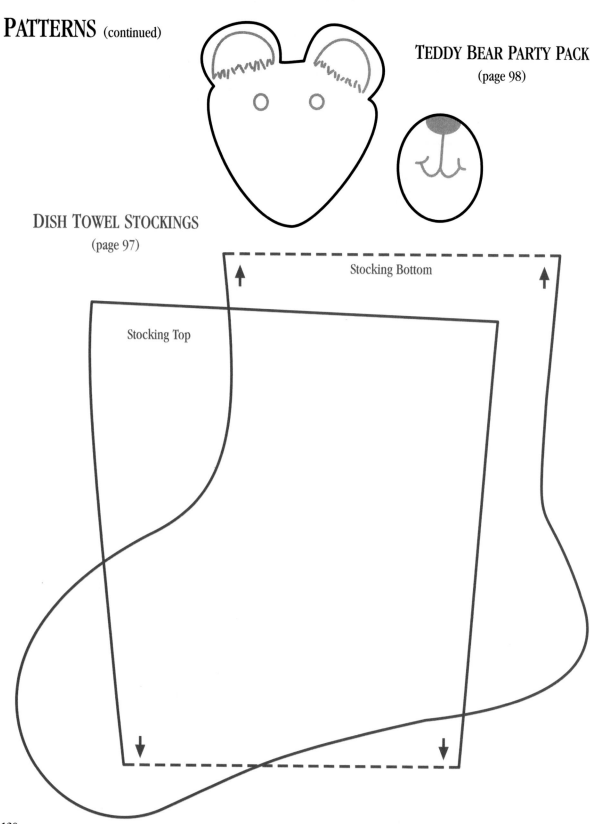

DISH TOWEL STOCKINGS
(page 97)

Stocking Bottom

Stocking Top

GENERAL INSTRUCTIONS

ABOUT THE PAPER WE USED

For many of the projects in this book, we used white and colored paper. There are a variety of papers for these projects available at copy centers or craft stores. When selecting paper, choose one that is suitable in weight for the project. We used copier paper, card and cover stock, construction paper, poster board, bristol board, and handmade paper.

ABOUT ADHESIVES

Refer to the following list when selecting adhesives. Carefully follow the manufacturer's instructions when applying adhesives.

CRAFT GLUE: Recommended for paper, fabric, wood, and floral items. Dry flat or secure with clothespins or straight pins until glue is dry.

FABRIC GLUE: Recommended for fabric or paper items. Dry flat or secure with clothespins or straight pins until glue is dry.

HOT/LOW-TEMPERATURE GLUE GUN AND GLUE STICKS: Recommended for paper, fabric, and floral items; hold in place until set. Dries quickly. Low-temperature glue does not hold as well as hot glue, but offers a safer gluing option.

CRAFT GLUE STICK: Recommended for small, lightweight items. Dry flat.

SPRAY ADHESIVE: Recommended for adhering paper or fabric items.

RUBBER CEMENT: Recommended for adhering paper to paper. Dries quickly.

DECOUPAGE GLUE: Recommended for applying fabric or paper pieces to smooth surfaces.

HOUSEHOLD CEMENT: Used for ceramic and metal items; secure until set.

COVERING A BOX

Use this technique to cover cardboard boxes that are unassembled or are easily unfolded, such as pie boxes.

1. Unfold box to be covered. Cut a piece of wrapping paper 1" larger on all sides than unfolded box. Place wrapping paper right side down on a flat surface.
2. For a small box, apply spray adhesive to outside of entire box. Center unfolded box adhesive side down on paper; press firmly to secure. For a large box, apply spray adhesive to bottom of box. Center unfolded box adhesive side down on paper; press firmly to secure. Applying spray adhesive to one section at a time, repeat to secure remaining sections of box to paper.
3. Use a craft knife to cut paper even with edges of box. If box has slits, use craft knife to cut through slits from inside of box.
4. Reassemble box.

MAKING A BASKET LINER

For liner with an unfinished edge, cut or tear a fabric piece 1/4" larger on all sides than desired finished size of liner. Fringe edges of fabric piece 1/4" or use pinking shears to trim edges.

For liner with a finished edge, cut a fabric piece 1/2" larger on all sides than desired finished size of liner. Press edges of fabric piece 1/4" to wrong side; press 1/4" to wrong side again and stitch in place.

MAKING A BOW

Loop sizes given in project instructions refer to the length of ribbon used to make one loop of bow.

1. For first streamer, measure desired length of streamer from one end of ribbon; twist ribbon between fingers (Fig. 1).

Fig. 1

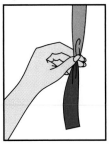

2. Keeping right side of ribbon facing out, fold ribbon to front to form desired-size loop; gather ribbon between fingers (Fig. 2). Fold ribbon to back to form another loop; gather ribbon between fingers (Fig. 3).

Fig. 2   Fig. 3

3. If a center loop is desired, form half the desired number of loops, then loosely wrap ribbon around thumb and gather ribbon between fingers (Fig. 4). Continue to form loops, varying size of loops as desired, until bow is desired size.

Continued on page 122

GENERAL INSTRUCTIONS (continued)

Fig. 4

4. For remaining streamer, trim ribbon to desired length.

5. To secure bow, hold gathered loops tightly. Fold a length of floral wire around gathers of loops. Hold wire ends behind bow, gathering all loops forward; twist bow to tighten wire. Arrange loops and trim ribbon ends as desired.

MAKING APPLIQUÉS

Follow all steps for each appliqué. When tracing patterns for more than one appliqué, leave at least 1" between shapes on web.

To make a reverse appliqué, trace pattern onto tracing paper, turn traced pattern over, and follow all steps using traced pattern.

When an appliqué pattern contains shaded areas, trace along entire outer line for appliqué indicated in project instructions. Trace outer lines of shaded areas for additional appliqués indicated in project instructions.

1. Trace appliqué pattern onto paper side of web. (Some pieces may be given as measurements. Draw shape the measurements given in project instructions on paper side of web.) Cutting about $1/2$" outside drawn lines, cut out web shape.

2. Follow manufacturer's instructions to fuse web shape to wrong side of fabric. Cut out shape along drawn lines.

MAKING PATTERNS

When entire pattern is shown, place tracing paper over pattern and trace pattern; cut out. For a more durable pattern, use a permanent pen to trace pattern onto stencil plastic; cut out.

When only half of pattern is shown (indicated by blue line on pattern), fold tracing paper in half and place fold along blue line of pattern. Trace pattern half; turn folded paper over and draw over traced lines on remaining side of paper. Unfold paper and cut out pattern. For a more durable pattern, use a permanent pen to trace pattern half onto stencil plastic; turn stencil plastic over and align blue line with traced pattern half to form a whole pattern. Trace pattern half again; cut out.

When patterns are stacked or overlapped, place tracing paper over pattern and follow a single colored line to trace pattern. Repeat to trace each pattern separately onto tracing paper.

PAINTING TECHNIQUES

TRANSFERRING A PATTERN

Trace pattern onto tracing paper. Using removable tape, tape pattern to project. Place transfer paper coated side down between project and tracing paper. Use a stylus or an old ball point pen that does not write to transfer outlines of basecoat areas of design to project (press lightly to avoid smudges and heavy lines that are difficult to cover). If necessary, use a soft eraser to remove any smudges.

PAINTING BASECOATS

A disposable foam plate makes a good palette.

Use a medium round brush for large areas and a small round brush for small areas. Do not overload brush. Allowing to dry between coats, apply several thin coats of paint to project.

TRANSFERRING DETAILS

To transfer detail lines to design, replace pattern and transfer paper over painted basecoats and use stylus or an old ball point pen that does not write to lightly transfer detail lines onto project.

ADDING DETAILS

Use a permanent pen to draw over detail lines.

SPONGE PAINTING

Use an assembly-line method when making several sponge-painted projects. Place project on a covered work surface. Practice sponge-painting technique on scrap paper until desired look is achieved. Paint projects with first color and allow to dry before moving to next color. Use a clean sponge for each additional color.

For allover designs, dip a dampened sponge piece into paint; remove excess paint on a paper towel. Use a light stamping motion to paint item.

For painting with sponge shapes, dip a dampened sponge shape into paint; remove excess paint on a paper towel. Lightly press sponge shape onto project. Carefully lift sponge. For a reverse design, turn sponge shape over.

SEWING SHAPES

1. Center pattern on wrong side of one fabric piece; use fabric marking pencil or pen to draw around pattern. Do not cut out shape.
2. Place fabric pieces right sides together. Leaving an opening for turning, carefully sew pieces together directly on drawn line.
3. Leaving a 1/4" seam allowance, cut out shape. Clip seam allowance at curves and corners. Turn right side out and press.

CROSS STITCH

CROSS STITCH (X)

Work one Cross Stitch to correspond to each colored square in chart. For horizontal rows, work stitches in two journeys (Fig. 1). For vertical rows, complete each stitch as shown in Fig. 2.

Fig. 1   Fig. 2

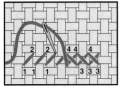

BACKSTITCH (B'ST)

For outline detail, Backstitch (shown in chart and color key by black or colored straight lines) should be worked after design has been completed (Fig. 3).

Fig. 3

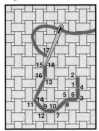

FRENCH KNOT

Bring needle up at 1 (Fig. 4); wrap floss once around needle and insert needle at 2, holding end of floss with non-stitching fingers. Tighten knot, then pull needle through fabric, holding floss until it must be released. For a larger knot, use more strands; wrap only once.

Fig. 4

WORKING ON WASTE CANVAS

1. Cover the edges of canvas with masking tape.
2. Mark center of desired stitching area on project with a pin. Match center of canvas to pin on project. With canvas threads straight, pin canvas to project; pin interfacing to wrong side. Baste all three thicknesses together (Fig. 5).

Fig. 5

3. Using a sharp needle, work design, stitching from large holes to large holes.
4. Trim canvas to within 3/4" of design. Dampen canvas until it becomes limp. Use tweezers to pull out canvas threads one at a time.
5. Trim interfacing close to design.

EMBROIDERY STITCHES

BLANKET STITCH

Bring needle up at 1; keeping thread below point of needle, go down at 2 and come up at 3 (Fig. 1). Continue working as shown in Fig. 2.

Fig. 1   Fig. 2

CROSS STITCH

Bring needle up at 1 and go down at 2. Come up at 3 and go down at 4 (Fig. 3).

Fig. 3

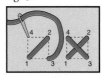

RUNNING STITCH

Make a series of straight stitches with stitch length equal to the space between stitches (Fig. 4).

Fig. 4

STEM STITCH

Bring needle up at 1; keeping thread below the stitching line, go down at 2 and bring needle up at 3. Take needle down at 4 and bring needle up at 5 (Fig. 5).

Fig. 5

STRAIGHT STITCH

Bring needle up at 1 and go down at 2 (Fig. 6). Length of stitches may be varied as desired.

Fig. 6

KITCHEN TIPS

MEASURING INGREDIENTS

Liquid measuring cups have a rim above the measuring line to keep liquid ingredients from spilling. Nested measuring cups are used to measure dry ingredients, butter, shortening, and peanut butter. Measuring spoons are used for measuring both dry and liquid ingredients.

To measure flour or granulated sugar: Spoon ingredient into nested measuring cup and level off with a knife. Do not pack down with spoon.

To measure confectioners sugar: Lightly spoon sugar into nested measuring cup and level off with a knife.

To measure brown sugar: Pack sugar into nested measuring cup and level off with a knife. Sugar should hold its shape when removed from cup.

To measure dry ingredients equaling less than 1/4 cup: Dip measuring spoon into ingredient and level off with a knife.

To measure butter, shortening, or peanut butter: Pack ingredient firmly into nested measuring cup and level off with a knife.

To measure liquids: Use a liquid measuring cup placed on a flat surface. Pour ingredient into cup and check measuring line at eye level.

To measure honey or syrup: For a more accurate measurement, lightly spray measuring cup or spoon with cooking spray before measuring so the liquid will release easily from cup or spoon.

TESTS FOR CANDY MAKING

To determine the correct temperature of cooked candy, use a candy thermometer and the cold water test. Before each use, check the accuracy of your candy thermometer by attaching it to the side of a small saucepan of water, making sure thermometer does not touch bottom of pan. Bring water to a boil. Thermometer should register 212 degrees in boiling water. If it does not, adjust the temperature range for each candy consistency accordingly.

When using a candy thermometer, insert thermometer into candy mixture, making sure thermometer does not touch bottom of pan. Read temperature at eye level. Cook candy to desired temperature range. Working quickly, drop about 1/2 teaspoon of candy mixture into a cup of ice water. Use a fresh cup of water for each test. Use the following descriptions to determine if candy has reached the correct stage:

Soft-Ball Stage (234 to 240 degrees): Candy can be rolled into a soft ball in ice water but will flatten when removed from water.

Firm-Ball Stage (242 to 248 degrees): Candy can be rolled into a firm ball in ice water but will flatten if pressed when removed from water.

Hard-Ball Stage (250 to 268 degrees): Candy can be rolled into a hard ball in ice water and will remain hard when removed from water.

Soft-Crack Stage (270 to 290 degrees): Candy will form hard threads in ice water but will soften when removed from water.

Hard-Crack Stage (300 to 310 degrees): Candy will form brittle threads in ice water and will remain brittle when removed from water.

SOFTENING BUTTER OR MARGARINE

To soften 1 stick of butter, remove wrapper and place butter on a microwave-safe plate. Microwave on medium-low power (30%) 20 to 30 seconds.

SOFTENING CREAM CHEESE

To soften cream cheese, remove wrapper and place cream cheese on a microwave-safe plate. Microwave on medium power (50%) 1 to 1 1/2 minutes for an 8-ounce package or 30 to 45 seconds for a 3-ounce package.

SHREDDING CHEESE

To shred cheese easily, place wrapped cheese in freezer 10 to 20 minutes before shredding.

TOASTING NUTS

To toast nuts, spread nuts on an ungreased baking sheet. Stirring occasionally, bake in a 350-degree oven 5 to 8 minutes or until nuts are slightly darker in color.

PREPARING CITRUS FRUIT ZEST

To remove the zest (colored outer portion of peel) from citrus fruits, use a fine grater or fruit zester, being careful not to grate bitter white portion of peel.

TOASTING COCONUT

To toast coconut, spread a thin layer of coconut on an ungreased baking sheet. Stirring occasionally, bake in a 350-degree oven 5 to 7 minutes or until coconut is lightly browned.

WHIPPING CREAM

For greatest volume, chill a glass bowl and beaters before beating whipping cream. In warm weather, place chilled bowl over ice while beating whipping cream.

SUBSTITUTING HERBS

To substitute fresh herbs for dried, use 1 tablespoon fresh chopped herbs for 1/2 teaspoon dried herbs.

CUTTING OUT COOKIES

Place a piece of white paper or stencil plastic over pattern. Use a permanent felt-tip pen with fine point to trace pattern; cut out pattern. Place pattern on rolled-out dough and use a small sharp knife to cut out cookies. (*Note:* If dough is sticky, frequently dip knife into flour while cutting out cookies.)

MELTING CHOCOLATE

To melt chocolate, place chopped or shaved chocolate in top of a double boiler over hot, not simmering, water. Using a dry spoon, stir occasionally until chocolate melts. Remove from heat and use as desired. If necessary, chocolate may be returned to heat to remelt.

EQUIVALENT MEASUREMENTS

1 tablespoon	=	3 teaspoons
1/8 cup (1 fluid ounce)	=	2 tablespoons
1/4 cup (2 fluid ounces)	=	4 tablespoons
1/3 cup	=	5 1/3 tablespoons
1/2 cup (4 fluid ounces)	=	8 tablespoons
3/4 cup (6 fluid ounces)	=	12 tablespoons
1 cup (8 fluid ounces)	=	16 tablespoons or 1/2 pint
2 cups (16 fluid ounces)	=	1 pint
1 quart (32 fluid ounces)	=	2 pints
1/2 gallon (64 fluid ounces)	=	2 quarts
1 gallon (128 fluid ounces)	=	4 quarts

HELPFUL FOOD EQUIVALENTS

1/2 cup butter	=	1 stick butter
1 square baking chocolate	=	1 ounce chocolate
1 cup chocolate chips	=	6 ounces chocolate chips
2 1/4 cups packed brown sugar	=	1 pound brown sugar
3 1/2 cups unsifted confectioners sugar	=	1 pound confectioners sugar
2 cups granulated sugar	=	1 pound granulated sugar
4 cups all-purpose flour	=	1 pound all-purpose flour
1 cup shredded cheese	=	4 ounces cheese
3 cups sliced carrots	=	1 pound carrots
1/2 cup chopped celery	=	1 rib celery
1/2 cup chopped onion	=	1 medium onion
1 cup chopped green pepper	=	1 large green pepper

RECIPE INDEX

CREDITS

We want to extend a warm *thank you* to Duncan and Nancy Porter for allowing us to photograph our Jelly-Filled Doughnuts in their home.

To Magna IV Color Imaging of Little Rock, Arkansas, we say *thank you* for the superb color reproduction and excellent pre-press preparation.

We want to especially thank photographers Larry Pennington, Mark Mathews, and Ken West of Peerless Photography, Little Rock, Arkansas, for their time, patience, and excellent work.

To the talented people who helped in the creation of the following projects in this book, we extend a special word of thanks:

- *Mug*, page 26: Linda Gillum
- *Strawberry Gift Collection*, page 36: Jane Chandler
- *Apron*, page 74: Sandi Gore Evans
- *Mini-Tote*, page 79: designed by Pat Olson, needlework adaptation by Christine Street
- *Cookie Basket*, page 84: Deborah A. Lambein